Paké: Writings by Chinese in Hawaii

Edited by Eric Chock & Darrel

Bamboo Ridge Press   1989

This is a special double issue of *Bamboo Ridge, The Hawaii Writers' Quarterly*, No. 42 and 43, Spring and Summer 1989, ISSN 0733-0308.

ISBN 0-910043-17-5
Copyright 1989 Bamboo Ridge Press
Indexed in the American Humanities Index
Indexed in the American Index of Periodical Verse

Published by Bamboo Ridge Press
Editors: Eric Chock and Darrell H.Y. Lum
Managing Editors: Mavis Hara and Kelly Okada
Cover and artwork: Doug Young
Design: Wendy Kim
Typesetting: Gail N. Harada

Some of the work in this issue has been previously published. A listing is included in the Acknowledgments.

Bamboo Ridge Press is a non-profit, tax exempt organization formed to foster the appreciation, understanding, and creation of literary, visual, audio-visual and performing arts by and about Hawaii's people. Tax-deductible contributions are welcomed.
Bamboo Ridge, The Hawaii Writers' Quarterly is supported in part by grants from the State Foundation on Culture and the Arts (SFCA). The SFCA is funded by appropriations from the Hawaii State Legislature and by grants from the National Endowment for the Arts. This issue is also supported in part by a grant from the National Endowment for the Arts (NEA) a federal agency.
Bamboo Ridge is a member of the Coordinating Council of Literary Magazines.
Subscriptions to *Bamboo Ridge, The Hawaii Writers' Quarterly* are available for $12 per year.

Bamboo Ridge Press
P.O. Box 61781
Honolulu, Hawaii 96839-1781

Library of Congress Cataloging-in-Publication Data

Paké : writings by Chinese in Hawaii / [edited by] Eric Edward Chock and Darrell Hoong Yip Lum.
    p.   cm.
ISBN 0-910043-17-5
  1. American literature--Hawaii.   2. American literature--Chinese American authors.   3. Chinese Americans--Hawaii--Literary collections.   4. Hawaii--Literary collections.   I. Chock, Eric Edward, 1950-   II. Lum, Darrell H. Y.
PS571.H3P35   1989
810.9'89510969--dc20
                          89-81392
                          CIP

Paké: Writings by Chinese in Hawaii

Contents

Introduction

What is a Paké Writer?   Eric Chock

When I was young, I always thought my father was a
typical Paké of his time. I remember how he could fix
things, like radios or TVs; or build things with his electric
saw and drill, like mahogany and glass cabinets and
linoleum top tables; or even if it took days, repair the old
family '50 Dodge, or the "new" '66 Dodge he still drives.
You might say he just didn't want to spend the money on
something new. But, he was an electrician, carpenter,
handyman, plumber, mechanic, who sells stocks today. He
learned how to manipulate the machines and tools of his
time, changed jobs in midstream, secured a home for his
family, and basically kept on top of things long enough to
be comfortable as he moves into old age. He was my role
model for what it meant to be a local Chinese, a paké.

Paké is the unique Hawaiian pidgin term for the
Chinese people. It is one of those words that we often
hear without knowing how it originated, what language or
languages it is derived from, or whether it is supposed to
be somehow descriptive of Chinese characteristics.
Nevertheless, we have a common understanding of the
word, and we use it from time to time, varying our usage
with situation and audience.

When asked to describe or define a local Chinese
writer, we often have a similar response. We are not sure
if the term is supposed to delimit certain characteristics of
style or theme, but still, the term is used occasionally,
sometimes changing with context.

In this collection, we attempted to publish the best
literature by a variety of writers of Chinese ancestry from
different times in Hawaii's history. Because we only looked
at works in English, our anthology includes writings
published from the 1920's to the present. Some works
have their roots in the time when Hawaii was still a
sovereign nation, but most span the territorial period
through Statehood. In other words, the Americanization of
Hawaii is the socio-political backdrop for this book.

It was therefore not incidental that themes of acculturation or assimilation or inter-generational conflict were prevalent in the 1920's to 1950's when many second or third generation Chinese were for the first time re-defining themselves in modern American ways. In fact, most of those earlier writings were done by University of Hawaii students who had established the Chinese Student Alliance and were clearly attempting to identify themselves as Americans to the community at large, and probably, to each other as well.

Many themes were worked out in stories of courtship and romance, leading a Romeo and Juliet kind of atmosphere to the many dramas with interracial pairings. These, and most of the other pieces, were also set in relation to families or close communities of Chinese in Hawaii. And though more of the modern pieces concern themselves with universal or non-ethnic themes, many still incorporate cultural customs or influences, again often in the context of the family, and why not! As paké, as Chinese Americans in Hawaii—like Americans of all cultural backgrounds—we are constantly re-defining and re-inventing our lives in an effort to expound and define and improve ourselves, just as our ancestors did in coming here.

Paké: Our Literary Tradition Darrell H.Y. Lum

It was just last year when a prominent English professor in defending his selection of writers for his anthology of stories about Hawaii said that the book was intended to be a collection of stories by "writers in English from the Western world." Thus, the omission of Chinese and Japanese American authors and others born in the islands was, in his eyes, understandable. Further, he lamented that there were many excellent but untranslated writings about the Pacific and he hoped to see more of them in print.

The notion of immigrant people having a literature written in English, being a part of the Western world and writing in the tradition of Western writers seems to be unheard of to most readers and to presumably well-educated and well-informed English professors. Yet, creative writing in English by Hawaii writers, immigrants and children of immigrants, has been around since the Islands joined the Western world a couple of hundred years ago. And not surprisingly, a large number of works written by high school and University students since the 1920s is readily accessible in various student annuals and literary journals in the Hawaii Pacific Collection in Hamilton Library at the University of Hawaii and in the Hawaii State Library.

Indeed, we *do* have a literary history: in English, with Hawaii settings, themes and concerns, in the Western literary tradition; literature that is lively and vibrant and concerns itself with making a contemporary Asian American life in Hawaii. These are not legends and fables of the "old country" nor the tales of immigrants yearning to return to the homeland. These are tales of settlers, making a life in the Islands struggling with the mix of cultures and generations and languages. Tales of generational conflict, of marrying outside of your own ethnic group, tales that use pidgin and Chinese and Japanese along with English, tales that were inspired by

10

Shakespeare and Eugene O'Neill as well as Chinese opera and radio melodrama are all a part of our literary history.

Yet we've been led to believe that we were somehow outside of the Western world; that we were without a literature or a literary tradition; that our capacity to express ourselves was somehow limited by the fact that our parents spoke another language or a pidgin; that we might speak a creole. One writer who attended the University in the 50s reported that he was advised in a creative writing course to make sure his characters were Haole and the settings were on the Mainland if he ever wanted his writing to amount to anything.

Despite these odds, literature was being written then and still is now. It still amazes local students that there exists a body of work by people like their parents or grandparents; that there might have been a poet, novelist, or playwright in their family. For as many detractors as there might have been, there have been those who nurtured writers and encouraged writing about people and topics close to home: Willard Wilson, English professor (who later served as Acting President of the University of Hawaii from 1957-58), encouraged his students to write about their own lives and had the foresight to carefully compile student scripts from 1936 to 1955 (in many cases, these original scripts are the only remaining copies); the students and advisers who put together the *Chinese Student Alliance Annuals* and the *Hawaii Quill Magazine*, which included creative writing and, in the case of the Quill, sponsored an annual writing contest; and others who encouraged young writers to put the concerns of their own lives down on paper. Some of the writing, as some authors modestly put it, were simply class assignments, first attempts and unpolished pieces. It was these young writers, some who were graduates of the English Standard School (and presumably encouraged to conform to strict standards of spoken and written English) who told their stories by forging a new literature based on the Western tradition using the circumstances and language (including pidgin!) of their own lives. As one early writer, when

11

asked why she chose to write in pidgin, said, "I wanted to make it real."

*****

As for the writers in this volume, their work is not easily pegged. This is not a volume about being Chinese in Hawaii, rather it is work by Hawaii's Chinese. And it defies easy categorizing. One poet declined to submit anything to us for fear that it would be published in a book with a cover that was primarily red with bamboo lettering and because he felt his work wasn't "Chinese-y" enough. We never intended it to be that anyway. We could never say which of our experiences or writings defines being Chinese in Hawaii. And we're not above laughing at ourselves—check out Eric Chock's poems "What? Another Chinese Holiday?!" as he complains about trying to figure out Moon Festival (after all, he's only half Chinese). And as we all struggle to deal with Moon Festival, Ching Ming, Chinese New Year and what we're supposed to do, we're consciously trying to preserve a Chinese tradition that is not truly Chinese to begin with, rather one that has evolved over the years and very likely bears little resemblance to anything done in China. A case in point is the banning of fireworks in Honolulu a few years ago which turned up an uproar of cultural and religious objections from those who I *know* popped firecrackers mainly for its incendiary thrill. Years of setting off strings of ten and twenty thousand crackers under the guise of culture and good luck bears little resemblance to anything done in China these days. The same goes for the lion dancing for dollar bills at weddings. This, too, is one of those uniquely Chinese-in-Hawaii traditions.

What we have is a *local* Chinese tradition that is our own. A tradition that acknowledges our history and debt to those early writers who made it possible for all of us to tell our stories.

So do all the writers in this volume share this view? Perhaps, but probably not. The fact of the matter is that whether we are Chinese, Chinese-Japanese, Chinese-Korean, Chinese-married-to-haole and we may not write with this particular identity in mind, we acknowledge that being Chinese is part of the equation that cannot be cancelled out.

The last time I went to Manoa Cemetery at Ching Ming, I teased my cousins about what it would be like when we were in the ground: Would our children brings us five containers from McDonalds and pour fruit punch and beer for us instead of gin and tea? We laughed but somehow we didn't doubt that they would do something. Like my putting a mooncake on my father's gravestone and bowing three times during the last Moon Festival. I suspect he knew I would be doing something (probably wrong), but *something*, nonetheless. I don't exactly know why I did it. It's just a part of who I am.

I don't exactly know why artist Doug Young turns to images of Chinatown and canned goods on a Chinatown store shelf to venerate. But we seem to still feel the pull of those early immigrants, no matter how far removed we get from them.

The selections in this book are about as diverse as the people. For lack of a better method, we've arranged the selections by birthdate of the author to give the reader some sense of time. We should be careful to point out however, that a number of the works were selected from student publications *Chinese Students Alliance Annual, Hawaii Quill Magazine*, and from compilations of scripts in *College Plays*. These were written and published while the authors were students at the UH or entrants in a writing contest. Some in fact were class assignments and many of the writers were surprised that we had dug them up. Thus some of the material needs to be read in light of not only when it was written but the age of the author at the time. Readers might be particularly interested in the similarities and differences in the three plays we've included. "The Submission of Rose Moy" written in 1928, "For You a Lei" in 1937, and "These Unsaid Things" in 1948 are approximately ten years apart and differ in significant ways. Yet the fundamental themes are remarkably similar. All three involve a parent-child generational conflict: conflict in cultures (American vs. traditional Chinese), conflict between characters' education and values (educated characters vs. less educated parents) and conflict in communication. The parents in all three plays are depicted rather harshly and "Rose Moy" and "Unsaid Things" have daughters who are about to leave home. The resolutions, some twenty years apart, are completely opposite, but sympathy toward the young, college-age characters is clear.

Three other selections, two stories by James Chun and Phoebe Chun Chang's "Li Po in Hawaii" were also written in the 1920s while the authors were students at the University. "Li Po" is a cleverly imagined visit to Hawaii by the wine-drinking classical Chinese poet of the Tang Dynasty whose observations are remarkably applicable today. James Chun's "Will of the Gods" deals with the problem of arranged marriage (the same dilemma of Rose Moy) in a comic way while still underscoring the traditional vs. modern theme. And "In the Camp" is one of the only depictions that we have of plantation life of the early Chinese immigrants.

The generational differences are also evident in some of the family history selections. Bessie Lai's contribution is taken from a book published in 1976, *Ah Yā, I Still Remember* which details the life of the earliest Chinese immigrants since her grandfather's arrival in 1859. Contrast her family history with the more recent ones of the Changs, the impressionistic glimpses of a youngest son in Joseph Chang's "Scenes from Childhood: Palolo Valley" and the family history as told by older brother, Thomas.

This theme, for the most part, disappears as we move to more recent work. The distance from the first generation has created perhaps a more romanticized depiction. Gone are the harsh views of the first generation, replaced by a veneration, a yearning that we might have known them better. The uniformly positive depictions of parents and grandparents by the younger writers Eric Chock, Wing Tek Lum, Cathy Song, Dana Yuen, Kathleen Young, and myself are almost the antitheses of the earlier works. There's a sense of loss of history or at least missing parts of history in this bicentennial year of Chinese in Hawaii. Two hundred years, nearly, the age of our nation, yet how much do we know of these 200 years? This literary tradition, as imperfect as it may be, still needs to be nurtured, taught, and read for it to continue.

This is not to say that the earlier writers stopped writing after college. Li Ling-Ai (who published under the name of Gladys Li in the *Quill*) is perhaps best known for her book, *Life is for a Long Time* (Hastings House, 1972), and Reuben Tam has capped a successful writing and painting career with the Cades Award this year.

And if some of the selections don't seem to be Chinese or Chinese in Hawaii at all, it's because that too is who we are. The national acclaim for poet Cathy Song or romance novelist Laureen Ching Kwock attests to their ability to reach audiences beyond these shores.

What is clear in much of the writing is the preponderance of family topics and themes. And as clear and distinct each voice is, what emerges is a sense of family and community and place. The net effect is, I think, one of appreciation for all of the outstanding writers and writing that this collection represents. And indignation that it took so long to recognize.

There are a number of people who need to be acknowledged for their efforts in producing this issue: Wing Tek Lum, researcher, Mavis Hara, managing editor, and Gail Harada. Many of the selections in this book were culled from the work of Stephen H. Sumida and Arnold T. Hiura's *Asian American Literature of Hawaii: An Annotated Bibliography*, (Hawaii Ethnic Resources Center: Talk Story, Inc., 1979).

Excerpt from
Ah Yā, I Still Remember   Bessie C. Lai

The Shrine of Saint Lee Yong

One night a Mrs. Fong, an especially kind woman
and resident of Happy Valley, dreamed that she was sitting
in her old rocking chair on the lanai of her home. A
stranger dressed in a long, dark robe appeared and spoke
to her in Chinese. "Madam, your precious daughter, Oe
Oe, is very ill and I have come to help her for I know who
will be able to cure her!" He pointed his finger up to the
sky toward the east and said, "Look up there, Madam!"
Mrs. Fong turned and looked up in the direction he was
pointing. There in the sky she saw three men standing
together and looking down at her. All of them wore long,
beautiful, and ornate Chinese robes. The stranger spoke
again and said, "Those three men whom you now gaze
upon are saints from heaven. The one standing in the
middle is the great and good Saint Lee Yong. It is he to
whom you must make your supplications for help because
he is the one who can cure your daughter."

Mrs. Fong then began to tell her neighbors of her
strange dream. She closed her story by stating, in a voice
that revealed her despair, "I suppose it is because I worry
so much about my poor Oe Oe that I dreamed such a
dream full of hope."

One of the elderly men in the group who had
listened intently and sympathetically to Mrs. Fong's story
said, "If this were China, we could make contact with the
saints in heaven and ask them to help Oe Oe. But here in
the Hawaiian Islands, so far away from China, our saints
and our God have lost track of us and do not know where
to find us." He sat shaking his head in negative doubt.

"Why can't we try it?" said another man. Then still
another, the eldest man in the group, spoke. His name was
Dang and he related his experience and teachings in
contacting saints while he was in China. "When I was a

young boy, the miracle brush and sand table were used in the shrine of my village." After a lengthy discussion, a plan was developed. It was later to be evidenced that the old man, Dang, was the only one of the twenty-two members of the shrine who could hold the miracle brush and commune with the saints. Ah Yā said that according to the Chinese wise men, one must have "sun-gut-chai" (certain perfect organs and body structure) in order to contact saints from the other world. Dang agreed to attempt spiritual contact and a meeting of the Chinese under the monkeypod tree was scheduled for early the next morning. All haste must be made if Oe Oe was to be saved!

Early that evening, all was in readiness. The table with a layer of white sand on the bottom was placed on the small enclosed porch of Dang's home. The brush holder was affixed and a stool positioned for Dang who was to operate the brush. An ornamental bowl was filled also with fine, white sand and placed on a table to be used as an altar. Four men had been chosen to perform the ritual. One was a "caller" who called out the Chinese characters which would be written on the sand table. He was selected because of his ability to read Chinese quickly and accurately. The next one had to write well and quickly for he had to record on paper everything the "caller" said. The third man was responsible to maintain vigilance at the altar and importune the saints for help. Dang, of course, was the fourth and operated the brush pen in its holder over the sand table.

The men had meticulously cleansed themselves with a bath and the community's faithful Chinese were gathered around the outside of the small porch in hopeful anticipation. All was ready. Three incense joss sticks were lighted and placed in the center of the bowl of sand. A pair of red candles was also lit and placed one on each side of the joss sticks. Dang took his place at the table and grasped the pen holder. After a few moments of intense concentration and perfect silence, Dang felt his hands being pulled in different directions and the onlookers were filled with excitement. They knew some contact was being made with the spiritual world! But when Dang paused and the inscriptions on the table were viewed, there was disappointment. There were only lines, circles and funny faces on the sand table. No intelligent contact had been made. Dang directed that incense papers be burned; two small sacred papers and two large sacred papers to dismiss the unwanted spirit they had contacted. They then tried the ritual again for several hours, but at every attempt were disappointed with their contacts.

Finally, the old man, Dang, slapped his forehead and remarked with great humility that he had forgotten something. He announced to the wearying congregation that he needed "Hoo Yan," a certain printed symbol that he recalled from his experience in China and proceeded to describe. Two young men who worked in a Chinese grocery store were sitting near Dang. One remarked, "If that is a sacred symbol and is called 'Hoo Yan,' it is a very strange coincidence. In every carton of Chinese tea we receive from Canton, there are at least two of these symbols printed on a piece of paper." The two were sent running to the store to obtain the "Hoo Yan." When the owner of the store was told the story of what his friends were doing, he opened every carton of Chinese tea he had and gave the young men all of the "Hoo Yan" symbols. Thanking him, the two ran back to where Dang and the others were patiently waiting.

Immediately, one of the "Hoo Yan" sacred symbols was burned and contact with a spirit began. But there were no Chinese characters on the table, only pictures and writing which no one could understand. Dang announced that he had a spirit that did not know how to write because each time a question was asked, the spirit tried to answer by drawing pictures. After several more contacts, a different spirit answered their call. Then, after a while, the following intelligible message appeared:

"What do you people want of me? I am not a saint. I am just an ordinary spirit; but because you burned the "Hoo Yan," someone had to answer your most persistent calls. I happened to pass by and was obligated to do so."

The man at the altar asked the spirit if the saint in Mrs. Fong's dream could be contacted because her daughter, Oe Oe, was very ill and needed help rapidly. The spirit replied, "This much I can tell you. In order to contact the saint, you must first contact one of the four "Too Dees" (earth governors).

The "Hoo Yan" was burned and the man at the altar pleaded that the "Too Dee" of the west come to their assistance. Soon the brush pen began to move and the caller read aloud: "I am the 'Too Dee' of the west. My name is Cheong and I am the oldest of all the Chinese people to die in the Hawaiian Islands. What do you people want?" The man at the altar said aloud that they wanted to contact the saint who had appeared in Mrs. Fong's dream. The "Too Dee" replied, "The saint you wish to contact is Saint Lee Yong. He is not here in the Hawaiian Islands but somewhere in China. I will fetch him for you." The people watched the clock and within three minutes the "Too Dee" announced that Saint Lee Yong was on his way.

Shortly, Dang's hands moved violently as he held the brush pen. Indeed, Saint Lee Yong was present. He introduced himself and conveyed the message that, in Chinese, he was "Lee Yong Tai Sin" (Tai Sin meaning great saint). He had been born long ago in Eastern China, was a doctor but had died as a young man.

He said he would remain available to the Chinese of Happy Valley as long as he was needed and that he would teach them "The Way." When the Saint had finished, the representatives conducting the ritual knelt down and asked him to help Oe Oe.

Saint Lee Yong replied that he would help Oe Oe. He knew she was a good girl and had always respected her parents and had been kind to them. He then prescribed a number of certain herbs which were to be mixed and from which tea was to be made and given to Oe Oe. She was to eat some sweet grapes with the tea. The saint was also advised that Oe Oe's uncle was very sick. He therefore prescribed a different combination of herbs from which tea was to be made. The uncle was advised to eat a ripe pear with the tea. With that, the brush pen stilled and the long, eventful day was concluded.

The next morning, Saint Lee Yong's prescription was followed. Oe Oe was given grapes and herb tea. Miraculously, as soon as she had drunk the tea and eaten the grapes, Oe Oe arose from her sickbed for the first time in weeks. Her mother knew that she was well and that the saint had helped her. Daily thereafter, Oe Oe continued to get stronger and more active. It was a matter of only a few days until she was fully recovered. Likewise, Oe Oe's uncle fully recovered after taking the cure prescribed by the Saint. Many, many people, hearing of the miracle, now came every evening to the little enclosed porch of Dang's home. They came for various reasons. But whether for curiosity or to be healed, they came and Dang realized something had to be done.

"Let us build a shrine and keep Saint Lee Yong here to help the people," he told the congregation one evening. Everyone agreed and one man volunteered to draw up the plans for constructing a shrine. There were no funds for materials, so another man passed the hat around immediately and everyone was surprised when the count totaled over fifty dollars from just the few people there!

Now in those days, fifty dollars was a lot of purchasing power and much lumber was bought to start the work. Thus the construction of the Shrine of Saint Lee Yong was begun. Excitement and happiness pervaded the Chinese community and after word spread of Oe Oe's miraculous recovery, the support for construction of the shrine grew. Monetary donations increased and labor was given freely. Everyone who could hold a hammer or saw pitched in willingly to do his share of the work. Harmony and happiness, cooperation and deeper community relationships grew.

Miracle Cures—Spiritual Cures

My Ah Yā (father) told a story frequently about the

cranky old man, Don Hon. He had retired from work long before this incident happened and lived in Hana, Maui, with his family. One day he arrived in Wailuku after a long and arduous trip on horseback. Don Hon was going to visit friends in Wailuku and proceed to nearby Kahului for a steamship trip to Honolulu. His purpose in this extensive travel was to see a physician in Honolulu in hopes he might be cured of suffering from arthritis, rheumatism and lumbago. He suffered terribly, not being able to sleep at night and becoming so cranky and irritable therefrom that no one could stand to be around this unpleasant man.

While in Wailuku, members of the shrine approached him with an offer to try the saint's cure.

Don Hon was as tired of being bombarded with saint stories as with anything else and said, "All right, I will for once be crazy and listen to you stupid fools!"

The following evening, when the faithful members assembled in the shrine, Don Hon's case was placed first on the list. Saint Lee Yong said that because of his age and the climate, Don Hon was suffering from a severe illness. The saint prescribed some specific herb leaves and roots of different plants to be boiled in a large pot of water. He cautioned to follow his instructions precisely in order for Don Hon to get well. First, before sunrise, Don Hon was to get a large pail of cold water from the nearby valley stream and soak his feet and legs in it for one-half hour. Then, at three o'clock in the afternoon, he was to boil the herb leaves and roots for one and one-half hours. While it was still very hot, he was to take a soak bath in it, being attentive to thoroughly soak those parts of his body most painfully afflicted.

Don Hon followed the instructions, he thought correctly, but that night he had no relief at all. Conversely, he ached and hurt more than ever. When the members came to visit him that evening, they found him red from both fury and the lengthy steaming he had gone through in the herb pot. Don Hon screamed and cursed at them for wasting his time, delaying his trip to Honolulu and trying to steam him like a crab or lobster. "Why did I let you people lead me into such nonsense!" he shouted, and over again he repeated, "If dead saints cure people there certainly are a lot of living doctors who will starve to death! How stupid, how dumb can I be to believe you idiots!" The members of the shrine present and bearing the brunt of Don Hon's wrath felt very badly and quietly departed to the shrine to commune with Saint Lee Yong.

They told the saint that the cure he had prescribed for Don Hon did not help him at all, to which the saint replied: "The medicine prescribed was correct and will cure him. Don Hon's timing was off. Go and ask him what time it was that he soaked his legs in the cold water of the mountain stream and at what time he boiled the herb and root medicine for his steam bath. Tell Don Hon to try again and to follow my directions. That you may believe and maintain your faith in me because you have asked me to help, I will."

Early the next morning, the members went to Don Hon and told him what the saint had said. To their relief, he admitted that he had not followed the instructions exactly. He said, "I know I was told to soak my feet and legs in the cold water before sunrise. However, when I felt how very cold it was, I said to myself, "This is insanity to suffer discomfort at this time of day," so I waited until the afternoon. I also did not boil the herb medicine at three o'clock in the afternoon, but waited and did it right before bedtime."

"Well," said one of the members, "what then can you expect? You criticize your friends and the saint unjustly for your own failures. We will help you if you agree to try it again and then the exact timing will be confirmed."

"I agree," said Don Hon by this time somewhat subdued.

Long before sunrise the next morning, a volunteer went to the cold mountain stream and obtained a large pail of the icy water. Awakening Don Hon, the cranky fellow's limbs were plunged into the frigid water amidst great rumblings of protest. Then, promptly at three o'clock in the afternoon, the herb and root medicine was placed on the stove to boil for the prescribed time. When it was ready, again a grumbling Don Hon was made to take his hot steam bath.

All through that night and the next morning, Don Hon could not believe what was happening. His suffering was gone; the pain and extreme discomfort had vanished! He was completely cured! When his friends came to visit him, he was smiling and full of joy. He kept saying over and over, "I don't believe it, but a miracle has happened. It is true; the saint has cured me!" He apologized profusely to his friends for insulting them and for making fun of Saint Lee Yong.

The members asked Don Hon if he would like to come and thank Saint Lee Yong personally at the shrine that evening. He was very willing and anxious to thank the saint for relief from his suffering. When the shrine opened that evening, Don Hon was instructed to bless himself upon entry with the holy water. He was then told to observe the "kow-tow" procedure and to repeat it before the altar. Soon, through the media of the sand table, Saint Lee Yong expressed his appreciation for Don Hon's presence and the humility he exhibited. Don Hon thanked the saint over and over and expressed his genuine appreciation for what the saint had done. He also requested forgiveness for his ignorance.

"Don Hon, would you like to hear of your past? The good and the bad you have done?" queried Saint Lee Yong.

A surprised Don Hon responded, "I have no religion, nor have I ever gone to church or been in a temple. I would very much like for you to comment on my good and bad and give me advice on what I should do."

"Over fifteen years ago," began Saint Lee Yong, "you did unjust and mean things to people. Over sixty people died or committed suicide because of your meanness. But you also did three years of good deeds. The good and bad were reviewed by "Yuk Wong Tai Dai," the Jade King, Almighty God, in heaven. If you had not done those three years of wonderful, good deeds to offset the bad deeds, I am afraid you would have been the eternal guest of Saint Yim Wong in hell when your soul departed the earth. Those unfortunate souls who died because of you would have taken their revenge for all the hereafter. I leave this to your thinking, Don Hon."

Don Hon got to his feet, took a large handkerchief from his pocket and wiped the abundant perspiration from his face. He walked out of the shrine followed by an amazed congregation of friends and the curious. Soon he was avalanched with questions about what he had done that was so bad and so good. The people fell silent as Don Hon began to tell his story.

"Over fifteen years ago, as many of you know, I was the big 'luna' (foreman) for one of the largest sugar plantations on Oahu owned by one of the richest Chinese. At that time, my family was large and I had to retain my job. I had to make sure that all of the Chinese laborers who came to the plantation as workers under three- and five-year contracts went to the sugarcane fields every day. Many were sick and at first I took it easy on them until one day, the boss corrected me. He told me to be sterner. Because I had good knowledge of the sugar plantation operations, he kept me as foreman. I thought the workers were no good—that they were playing sick and that they were lazy and I decided to solve the problem once and for all.

I went immediately and hired twelve of the meanest Hawaiian boys I could find. I gave them whips and set them upon the laborers every day. I intended to whip this laziness and false sickness out of them. The boys I hired were very, very mean. Naturally, all of the laborers resented me. They were whipped for almost no reason and many of the genuinely sick died as a result of the forced labor. I myself heard many of their last words—that they would never forget me and that I would be punished for my sins. After more than sixty of these souls perished from mistreatment and overwork, the boss fired me."

"What did you do for the following three years that

were so full of good deeds?" asked one of the members.

Don Hon thought pensively for a while and then said, "As many of you know, I came to Wailuku and loafed for a while. I had no money and it was at the time the Mauilani Hospital was just opening. The hospital needed volunteers to help out. Mr Tom, one of the merchants, said to me one day, 'Why don't you help? You can be a cook. It is better than just loafing around. The pay isn't much—$20.00 a month—but that will pay for your room rent and give you a few dollars to spend each month. Besides, you will be doing a great service for the sick and injured people of the community.' So I accepted the position and I worked hard for exactly three years. Not only did I cook, but I served and fed those who could not feed themselves. These must be the three years of good deeds that saint described. Had I known I was doing such good deeds, I would have worked longer!"

Don Hon vowed that from then on he would do all the good deeds he could, even if he could not enter heaven when he died. The next evening in the shrine, Saint Lee Yong spoke to Don Hon and the congregation:

"You have made a good confession to God and your friends, Don Hon. Your sins are forgiven and you will, someday, be welcome in heaven. It is unfortunate that many of your countrymen suffered at your hands."

Two years passed and Don Hon never for a moment suffered any of the pains from his former ailments. He was a faithful member of the shrine and an outstanding member of the community. One day, Saint Lee Yong knew that his lifespan was nearly up on earth, but because of his good deeds, the saint wrote on the sand table that he was granting Don Hon an extra ten good months of life. He was advised by the saint to take advantage of this time, leave the Hawaiian Islands and return to China for a visit with his relatives and to pay respect to the tombs of his ancestors. Don Hon did so, but because he corresponded with my Ah Yā, we all knew he lived ten years instead of ten months. The saint had meant ten

years when he wrote on the sand table, but the reader had
read the symbol as ten months.

In the Camp
James II. Chun

During the summer vacation I always returned to the
country store, and often I climbed into Ah Fat's delivery
wagon and accompanied him in his rounds to the
plantation camps. This time we were on our way to Camp
17 with a heavy load of groceries and a few letters. The
sun beat down with such heat that it sent the perspiration
trickling down our faces; the mule foamed and sweat over
the red, dusty road; the wagon rumbled and jolted
monotonously; the unvarying fields of cane seemed to
stretch on forever. After I had tried almost everything I
could to keep from dozing off, I took out the letters and
looked over them. All the names were unfamiliar to me
except one which was addressed "My son Wong Mun Sing;
from mother Wong."

Wong I remembered well, for occasionally he came
down the store and brought me mangoes or papayas. He
was about twenty-five, strong, good-looking, with an
unusually pleasant face, sprightlier than any of his
companion workers.

"Here is a letter from China for Wong Mun Sing," I
turned to my companion beside me. "Do you remember
him?"

"Yes, everybody does. He's the best worker in the
camp," he replied lazily without raising his sleepy eyes, the
reins loose on his lap, and his body rocking to and fro
with the movement of the wagon.

"That's why he got sick," he added as an
afterthought.

"Sick?" How did he get sick?"

"Worked too hard. Went to work during the rain
storm."

"Has he been sick long?"

"He was in bed the last three times I was up there."

Fat was not given to talking, especially not in a hot
and sleepy day. We rode on in silence; the only life being
disturbed were the doves we frightened up on the lonely

road.

"We're in Camp 17," he broke the silence as we passed a sharp turn and came to half a dozen drab-colored wooden buildings that stood out dull and sordid among a field of cane. The place, far away and hidden from any other human habitation, was lifeless. No children's voices to fill the air; no women's hands to wipe away the ugliness and dirt. Only the barking of a dog greeted our arrival. Some chickens wandered about aimlessly and a few pigs grunted and rolled in the mire of the pen.

Sounds in the kitchen drew us to the kitchen where we found the cook washing some cabbage for dinner. He unlocked the store-room for Ah Fat, and took the letters I offered him. After glancing at them, he said hastily, "Here, you'll find Wong in the second house," and handed one back to me.

The second house faced the kitchen. On the porch were flung here and there some mud-caked shoes and wooden slippers; some old straw hats that had lost their shape clung to the wall, and a brown bamboo pipe rested in a corner. The interior was dimly lighted, hot, suffocating. On both sides were arranged ten bunks which were simply boards placed on benches and covered with straw mats. Soiled clothing hung carelessly along the wall and articles were thrown in disorder. On a bunk in one corner Wong lay with closed eyes, curled up under a thick blanket that badly needed washing. Before him was a tray on which a little oil lamp burned dimly, and by its side slept a dark pipe.

As I approached he opened his eyes, and recognizing me as the storekeeper's son, he said he was glad to see me. But his voice was weak and his eyes lacked their old sparkle.

"Have you been sick a long time, Mr. Wong?" I asked with respect as I took one of the scanty pieces of furniture, a kerosene box, to the side of the bed to sit on.

"Quite a while, but I'm getting better now," he answered weakly.

"I'm glad you are better. Here is a letter for you," I

added.

"A letter for me?" he broke out in surprise. "From whom could it be!"

"From China. From your mother, according to the envelope."

"Mother!" and a light shone in his eyes for just a moment. "Yes, mother!" he seemed to mutter to himself. "When will I see you again?"

Then he addressed me eagerly, "Tell me what she says, please."

I was rather glad to have the opportunity of doing something for him, so tearing the envelope I read: "My dear son, we are all well here, so let not your heart be worried on our account. But you have been away from home, separated from us by mountains and sea for many years, and we look forward for your return. Yuk Ung has been waiting all this time and longs for you to come back to make her happy. Your expectant mother."

Wong writhed under his coverlet as he listened, and an expression of pain passed over his worn face. For some moments he stared gloomily, dreamily, across the room.

"Damn all this!" he burst out suddenly with such vehemence that startled me. He grasped the edge of his bed tightly, his eyes became hard and desperate, and the blood rushed to his face and crimsoned it for a moment. "Damn this rotten work; and the cursed luck!"

"It must be a hard life," I ventured to put it.

"It's a ceaseless grind that squeezes the life out of you. Seven years have I been here and I'm not free from it yet." After a little while, losing his fire, he advised sympathetically, "My friend, you are young. Make use of your opportunity and get all the education you can and then you won't have to drudge like us old people."

"Why don't you save some money and get out of this?" I asked.

"I can't. I've saved every cent I could. Altogether it amounted to six or seven hundred dollars all these years. I thought two years more I will be able to see her and mother again."

"Two years is not so bad."

"But the trouble is—"

"What?"

"Now I can't get away in two years. This illness put me back more than a hundred and it'll be a long time before I can save that up again," and his eyes again had that hopeless stare.

"You'll have to wait longer, dear girl," he groaned. Noticing my puzzled look, he made an effort to edge closer to me and spoke very softly. "I have a mother and a wife back there—the sweetest girl—we were married just before I left for this cursed place. She is a faithful girl. But I never imagined I would be away so long."

He again fell into a spell of silence.

Finally he burst out again. "She must not wait too long."

"I don't believe you took opium before," I hinted and glanced at the tray and pipe by his side, knowing that a man in his position could not possibly save up and get away if addicted to the habit.

"No!" he said with a tinge of anger and shame in his voice. "No, only during my sickness, for it allays the pain in my head." After a while he added, "Let me tell you what. I'm going to cut this out as soon as I get well—as soon as I'm well."

I pitied him as I looked into his tired face—a young man in his prime, separated from his home and loved ones and unable to get back to them. By this time Ah Fat had finished a cordial pipe with the cook, had gotten his next order, and had discussed the prospects and price of the pigs, so he came in to say it was time to leave. All I could do was to bid farewell to the unhappy Wong, and went out again to the open air. On the way home, I sat depressed beside my companion and scarcely spoke to him, for my heart was full of grief and sympathy.

I did not have occasion to see my friend again until a very, very long time after. But I learned from Ah Fat sometime after my visit that he was well again and working in the fields. When I asked if he was still taking opium, Ah Fat said, "Of course he does. Don't expect anybody to give it up once he's gotten into it, especially when everybody else is smoking it. That's the only thing to drown their cares in their spare moments. And he joins in a game or two occasionally on a Sunday. Don't blame them. That's the only recreation those people have up there."

As time passed I almost forgot about him and the camp. And the next time I went there was some twelve years later, after I had finished a medical course in the mainland and made some success as a doctor. Ah Fat was still driving his one-horse wagon back and forth, but the changes of years were marked clearly on his tired features and form.

"I'd like to take a look at the old camps," I told him as he drove out from the shed on a Sunday.

"Jump on," he answered.

It was a hot day, so hot that it foreboded rain. That did not deter me however, so I clambered up the seat.

"We're going to Camp 17," he said as he slackened the reins. "Don't remember which one? Well—er—let me see, the one where Wong Mun Sing is. Don't remember him? Why, the one whom you saw sick one time."

"Oh, I remember. Is he still there? I thought he's gone to China by this time."

"He always wanted to go, but couldn't get enough money. Frequently he gets letters from China. I think I have one for him now."

As we talked to the weary rumbling of the wagon, we noticed that the weather was changing. Thick, dark clouds were gathering which soon covered the earth like a pall. The storm was approaching rapidly, so we urged the mule to a trot. By the time we reached the camp—which, with its cluster of desolate old buildings, the foundations of which were rotting in the sod, was a sorry disgusting spectacle—the rain was sweeping down from the far away mountains. We sought refuge in the nearest house. A confusion of noise and human voices met our ears. Around a large table, engaged in a game of pai gau, sat and stood a group of men—men in shirt sleeves, in blue shirts and black shirts, men in khaki trousers and in trousers of light stuff, men with wooden slippers or dirty shoes or men barefooted, men with overgrown hair and unshaven faces, men with pipes or without pipes, old men and young men, tall men and short men, but all with hard, sun-burnt faces. They did not pay much attention to us as we entered.

"Curse the luck!" swore he with the long hair.

"Luck! Wong's having all of it!" said he in shirt sleeves.

"I'm about cleaned up," added another.

"By the way he's going, he'll clean us up in no time," someone else put in.

"He must have cleared a couple hundred last night," observed the careless one with the pipe.

Sure enough, with a pile of bills and silver before him, sat Wong Mun Sing. But what a change! His face was lean and wrinkled, his cheeks hollow, his eyes sunken and ringed, and his hair gray. It seemed that he was only thirty-five or forty, but he appeared to be fifty or sixty.

"You fellows keep on going," he addressed the crowd. "I want to see somebody," he said, glancing toward me and raking up his winnings into his trouser pockets.

"Wait a while there! Give us a chance to get even," they all protested in unison.

"I'll be back in a while," he said and came toward me. His shoulders stooped slightly. He was no longer the young and strong man he used to be.

He said he was surprised to see me, but glad nevertheless. "And by Jove," he cried happily, "I've cleaned up quite a bunch these two days. Never had luck like this in my life before. I'll quit now, I guess, when the quitting's good." And he rushed away to his own lodging.

Outside the rain was pouring. It beat drearily upon the roof, dripped into the cracks and wet the walls within. It fell on the dirty porch, making it slippery and slimy. It flowed from the old clothes that hung on the line. It formed puddles of brown water in the yard, filled up the empty cans scattered about, and ran into the pig pens where the animals wallowed in mud and mire.

Inside the men were immersed in their game, unmindful of the storm outside. What is a little rain, anyway! Are they not used to it? But it must be a desolate and dreary life these people are leading. Work, always work, and little pleasure! The mud, the sweat and grime of it all! It was work under the burning afternoon sun and work amid the chilling rains of winter. There was no chance of a change, of going anywhere, enjoying any wholesome pleasure, no chance of seeing anybody but the same dirty companions. It was a hopeless drudgery and in their hearts they knew it. They aged and sickened before their time. Like the buildings that furnished them scanty shelter, their lives were mouldering away.

It was now nearing supper time, yet the rain continued its downpour. Suddenly voices across the yard rose above the patter of the rain. "Some one get the doctor quick!" Ah Fat rushed over bare-headed and pulled me to the second house.

"What's the trouble?" I demanded.

"Wong's gone crazy," he panted.

In the corner where I saw him before, lay Wong writhing and wriggling on his cot, his knotty claws clutching at the open air. Perspiration stood on his pale face. He hissed through his opium-stained teeth breaths that smelt of liquor and now and then he sent forth a shrill terrifying cry that drew everybody in the camp to his bedside. "I told you I was coming," he whined. "Now I am coming, right away. I have the money." With difficulty we succeeded in quieting him down. But his heart was beating weakly, and he was sinking. The effects of alcohol and the long use of opium were telling on him.

"It happened this way," one of the men explained, handing me a letter. Ah Fat brought this to him today. After he read it, he bought five dollars worth of opium and a bottle of liquor—he won plenty of money and could afford it. He must have taken the whole thing."

I took the letter. It was from China, not from his mother, but from someone unknown to me. The contents were very brief and ran something like this: "I am sorry to inform you that as a result of a long sickness, your wife has passed away."

Some of the men stood unmoved; some bent their heads in sympathy. Some of them knew that as they looked down on the gaunt face and large eyes of the dying man, they were looking into the same fate that was awaiting themselves. Gradually the crowd dispersed. The rain had now ceased; the gloom was deepening.

The eyes of the man on the bunk, too, lost its little remaining light. The heart that had borne so much grief beat no longer, and the body that had weathered so much toil lay motionless.

And from across the yard the clatter of cards and the jumble of voices again disturbed the stillness.

The Will of the Gods   James H. Chun

The thick mango trees in the yard were flooded with
the whistling notes of happy sparrows that were chirping
good-night to their companions. But across the lane, the
red and yellow temple remained quiet; the smoke of the
late afternoon incense, like the breath of some sleeping
monster, curled above it and evaporated into nothingness.
The lane was almost deserted, save that farther up, six or
seven Hawaiian and Chinese boys were shooting marbles
together, calling and shouting with the lustiness and joy of
growing childhood. An old woman emerged from the
temple with her brown bamboo basket and shuffled away
in her Oriental slippers.

For half an hour David and Marie had been standing
by the gate, lost to everything around them. She stood
within, picking with her smooth, round fingers, the petals
of a newly plucked rose from the bush in the yard. She
was a pretty maid, smart in her neat white dress, small but
not too small, easy, with soft black hair, and with depth
and fire in her dark eyes. He was big and full of energy,
his athletic figure enhanced by his white sweater and dark
trousers. His face was tanned, being so much exposed to
the sun in his work for the City and County Engineer
Department. It was one of those faces that are determined,
dauntless, and somehow inspire hope and optimism; and
his eyes seem to laugh and twinkle. These two ought to
make a handsome and happy pair, the children that
belong to the generation born and brought up under
Hawaiian skies.

But Marie did not seem to be happy at that moment.
She was excited; her eyes sparkled and the blood rushed
to her cheeks as she fired out her words. "Oh, David oh!
What shall I do? We must do something."

"This Lau Long fellow wants to marry you?" he
asked.

"Yes, today Kum Po came over with his offers. She
talked with Ma in the parlor and I overheard them."

37

"And your mother is favorably disposed to this man, Marie?"

"Ma is delighted with the offer. She has always wanted me to marry rich." She continued, "But I won't marry him!" as she crushed the flower in her hands.

"But your mother has not given her consent to this go-between woman yet, has she?"

"Not yet. But she intends to tomorrow. When she is set on anything, she doesn't give in either. She must go to the temple and consult the gods first. Mother is very reverent, or rather superstitious."

"Ugh." David passed his hands over his hair and knitted his brows.

"Does your mother believe in this temple stuff?" he asked.

"Believe!" she exclaimed. "Everything she does, she must first consult the gods. When anyone in the family is sick she goes to the temple. When sister married, she went to the temple, and one of her early suitors was turned down because the gods foreboded bad luck."

"And so tomorrow she's going to the temple to get advice in regard to your marriage. You're sure of that?"

"That's what she said."

Suddenly a voice rang out from the house. "Ah Heong! Ah Heong! Come in this minute!"

Marie was the name by which she was known to her youthful companions. To her mother and father she was Lin Heong, or for short, Ah Heong. Her last name was Ching.

"That's Ma calling," she explained.

"I was going to ask your mother for your hand, Marie," he added. "But I don't think that this is the psychological moment for it. However, I'll see her tomorrow."

"But you shouldn't do it yourself, Dave. That's not the way they do it, and you'll surely be turned down," she suggested.

"Don't worry!" His look gave her confidence.

"Now I must see what Ma wants."

David admiringly watched her disappear into the house. Then he crossed the lane toward the temple.

"That Tong Fun's son who has been talking to you?" Mrs. Ching spoke sharply as Marie entered. "He seems to be here pretty often lately. A girl like you shouldn't stay out talking to him. Don't you dare go out and encourage him any more. Now go and get supper ready, and after that I'll tell you something more to your good."

Mrs. Ching was a short and stout woman and she appeared doubly stouter in her wide dress and trousers. She really was not a stern woman although her tongue sounded sharp at times. Stubborn perhaps when once her will had been made up. A little too critical and watchful over Marie's affairs naturally, for she had her eye open for a good husband for her. Her philosophy conflicted with that of her educated daughter, of course, for she had been brought up within the four walls of an ancient home without the meagerest bit of formal education. Life to her was but a series of happenings ordained by Fate, and she swallowed and digested everything that tinged of the supernatural.

The parlor to which the family retired represented a conflict of taste. A few Eastern-made, teak wood chairs and a pair of Western-made wickers mixed up. A piano stood out boldly in one corner. On the wall some embroidered pieces of the eight fairies of old, the large characters "hook sau" in a gilded frame, meaning "blessings and long life," vied with pictures of Hawaiian scenery, and a black and gold pennant. The gorgeous table covering contrasted inharmoniously with the plain window curtains.

Marie sat before the piano, Father Ching slumped lazily into one of the wickers behind a newspaper, while Mother made herself comfortable in a teak wood chair.

"We have good reason to rejoice tonight, Ah Heong's pa," she began with a broad smile, "for this day the well-known Lau Long has bid for our daughter's hand."

Marie knew it was coming, so if she felt anything she did not show it. Ching looked up from his paper, shifted his glance from his wife to his daughter, and remarked simply, "He's rich enough. I suppose he's made a good offer." Ching was a man of reserve, something of a philosopher.

"Good!" exclaimed his wife. "I'd like to know who can make a better! Here is what Kum Po proposed. Listen! Four thousand cakes, a pair of roast pigs, two dozen chickens, four dozen bottles of mui kwai loo, five hundred dollars in gold, jewelry, clothes. What an elaborate wedding we shall enjoy! And won't it be the talk of the city!" She stopped for breath.

"A rich offer indeed," he acquiesced. "What do you think of him, Ah Heong?"

"I think he's a fool," she broke out.

"What?" exclaimed the surprised mother. "He's one of the richest men in the city."

"What of it? What do I care how rich he is! And they say he got his money smuggling opium. Anyhow I won't let myself be bought by the price he offers."

"Heh?" snapped the astonished Mrs. Ching. "What's that?"

"I won't marry that man," she continued, "I won't, and I won't."

"Heh? You won't? Who's going to decide whom you shall marry? I'll do it, not you."

"I'll marry only the man I love," Marie challenged defiantly.

"Oh!" Mrs. Ching was stunned. "Is she coming to this? Is that why that Tong boy has been coming here? Love!" she spoke contemptuously, "As if I married your father because I loved him at first! Look here, father, our daughter is throwing to the winds the teachings of our ancestors, turning kanaka right under our noses. That's what schooling has done for her—independence, liberty, nothing but disobedience!"

"Liberty is a good thing," commented Ching. "But it's like wine; too much of it makes you drunk—Now, daughter, you must listen to what your parents tell you. Obedience is the chief duty of a daughter."

"But I don't want to marry that old Lau. They say he's fifty. Ugh! Oh Pa," she lifted her pleading eyes to him, "would you sell me to him?"

"That's enough Ah Heong. Go to your room and we'll decide this ourselves," commanded Mrs. Ching. "I'll go to the temple tomorrow and ask the advice of the Kun Yum goddess. She'll tell us definitely what we should do."

Ching threw up his hands in defeat. "Hai, these modern girls with a little education are all the same, all the same. Like springs. The more you try to force them, the harder they fly back at you."

Marie threw herself on her bed, but for a long time she could not sleep. She shivered at the thought of having to marry Lau. When she awoke the next morning she was determined to rebel.

After her mother had made her preparations and gone, she, too, with a heavy heart, crossed the lane unobserved, climbed the flight of wooden steps of the temple, and slipped into an obscure corner where she could watch without being seen.

The artificiality and grotesqueness of the place disgusted her. The burning sticks of incense loaded the air with a fragrance that was choking. The smoke rose, spread, adding to the gloominess of the already ill-lighted precinct. The gilded letters, glittering woodwork, and colored hangings and lanterns, blushed shame-facedly from a rough and sordid background. On a blackened table rested the burners, gong, and a cylindrical bamboo container of prayer sticks. On finely carved pedestals, the dirty idols stared blankly into space. The yellow-faced and uneven legged priest hobbled delicately from the table to stand like a spineless chunk.

Mrs. Ching laid the meat and rice on the table, poured out the wine and tea, and lit the joss sticks and red candles. The priest drummed on the bronze gong a few clangs and then knocked on a hollow wooden box. The preliminary preparations were now completed.

Straining his head toward the table, for he must have been near-sighted, the priest picked up the pair of wooden dice, gahn bui, which resembled a banana cut lengthwise into halves, each with a flat and convex side. Kneeling before the images and bowing in mechanical obeisance, he mumbled a monotonous chant and asked for the consent of the beneficent Kun Yum pooh sard for the marriage of the daughter of Ching to the wealthy house of Lau.

Mrs. Ching looked on with a hopeful mien. Marie watched anxiously. The priest lifted his hand above his bowed head and cast the dice. They fell with a clack, rolled, and rested flat on the floor. It was an ominous sign! The priest lifted his hand and threw again, and again the dice fell flat. The third trial, and the same result. Mrs. Ching knitted her brows. Did the gods disapprove of such a marriage?

"Why doesn't one of these dice turn over on the other side?" she muttered.

Again and again the priest let fall the dice, but as often the same result greeted his efforts. Marie experienced a commotion of feeling, a mixture of awe, mysteriousness, and joy. She was puzzled. She wondered why the dice could be so consistent. Were the gods really helping her? The instinctive fear and awe for the supernatural seemed to get hold of her. Nevertheless she was glad!

Finally the priest looked up and turned to the now troubled woman beside him, "It is plain that the pooh sard looks with disfavor upon the marriage." Mrs. Ching stared dazedly at the priest.

The priest now took the tube of numbered sticks, and with both hands shook it before the idols, at the same time asking the gods to give their advice. In the shadows of the corner Marie held her breath. On this depended her fate. The stick that emerged from the tube would decide if she would have to marry Lau.

One of the sticks rose above the batch and dropped to the floor.

"Number 69," said the priest as he picked it up and stuck it close to his eyes, and then wrote the number on a piece of paper.

Number 69. She did not know what number 69 contained. She must wait.

Once more the sticks were reverently shaken, and this time the eighty-fifth emerged and fell to the ground.

"What do these fortunes say?" asked Mrs. Ching anxiously.

The priest slowly got to his feet. "The content of 69 is," he said, while Marie strained her ears to listen,

Hearken well to Heaven's gracious voice,
But let not riches bind the parents' choice,
For the silver moon remains not always round,
And cracks across the mirror will be found.

"And number 85 reads," he continued,

The son with wisdom, virtue, health,
Excels the one with ill-acquired wealth;
The snake in time will to a dragon change
And pierce to heaven, sea, and mountain range.

"So the Kun Yum goddess does not favor the match?" queried the beaten woman.

"No," he interpreted. "The gods do not favor Lau, but desire somebody else who is wise and strong."

"It is the pooh sard's will!" she murmured with bowed head.

Marie was jubilant. She slipped from her hiding-place, stole softly down the stairs, and walked briskly home with light steps, now convinced that the gods were on her side.

It was again near dusk. The fragrance of the rose and evening violet intermingled with the soft, cool air. The sparrows had nested and a reign of quietness prevailed. The breath of the temple was invisible now. Marie and David did not stand by the gate; they were sitting together on the step of the veranda.

A little while before that David had burst upon Mrs. Ching and asked for her daughter's hand and the latter had dropped the tea cup she was holding. After her astonishment she had consented.

"Kum Po did come for Ma's answer today," she was saying.

"And of course she didn't get your mother's consent," he added.

"No. She said the gods disapprove of the marriage." She added, "I disapprove of it more than they."

"And I too."

Silence ensued. A smile played about David's face, a smile that suggested happiness and amusement.

"What makes you keep smiling so tonight?" she asked.

"Why, Marie, I'm happy.—And by the way," he continued after a short pause, "did you see many persons go to the temple today?"

"Quite a number, including Ma. Why?"

"Oh, nothing much. Only they have my sympathy," he laughed.

"What do you mean?"

"They must have been given some bad fortune today; for the dice and the bottom ends of the prayer sticks except two were loaded with lead."

Li Po in Hawaii   Phoebe Chun Chang

The letters published here were supposed to have
been written by Li Po to his friend telling him what he
thought of the Hawaiian Islands. They were given by him
to a Star-Bulletin reporter, who went to interview him. "In
them," he said, "you will get my impressions while they
were fresh in my mind."

MY DEAR FU:
Here I am in this bewildering city where the people
rush from place to place without knowing where they are
going. My energy is greatly taxed trying to keep pace with
my surroundings. The ability to get the better of one's
neighbor seems to be a universal trait here. Thousands of
dollars are spent to place ads in the newspapers by stores
extolling the wonderful qualities of their goods. Posters
and placards cover every available space. "Use Pond's Cold
Cream for a Velvet Skin. Lady Windsor Uses It," or, "Ride
in a Ford, The Car of the People." To attract young
gentlemen, such lines appear as the following: "She will
appreciate a box of Moana Hawaiian Jams and Jellies."
Trusting young people would use the cold cream and
become sadly disillusioned. Young struggling workmen
and clerks would buy the Ford car and get killed by it
either physically or spiritually.
I once passed a restaurant which I think was called
the Tripoli Grill, although Tripoli is actually thousands of
miles away from here. The beautiful coloring and the
exquisite designs of its show windows attracted my
attention. On examining them more closely, I found the
most tempting dishes of lobster salads and fried fish and
lemon pie. And also there was an inviting sign board
which read, "Have your dinner here. Music while you eat."
I could not resist the temptation and so in I went. Soon I
was confronted with a tableful of foodstuff which my
stomach refused to take in and a bill which my
pocketbook could not cover. However, I got out of it by

45

inviting some passersby to come and dine with me and then left them there to pay for the repast.

At last I have escaped to the mountains away from the din and bustle of the city.

Why do I live in the mountains?
I laugh and answer not, my soul is serene,
It dwells in another heaven and earth belonging to no man,
The peach trees are in bloom and the river flows on—

I think it is about time for me to prepare for a picnic this evening, tomorrow I will tell you all about it.
Farewell.

MY DEAR FU:
There was a beautiful moon last night and the sky was cloudless. To make the atmosphere perfect I asked for a pot of wine. And those fools, can you imagine what they told me?

"It is a poison," one told me, "if you take it, it will make you flabby." "It will shorten your life by ten years," added another.

Three cups open the grand door to bliss,
Take a jug full, the universe is yours,
Such is the rapture of the wine.
That the sober shall not know.

The people who live in a land where wine drinking is a crime would never know the bliss drinking brings. A world without wine is like a night without the moon. As the moon lightens the darkness of the night so does wine lighten the sordidness and vexations of life.

With a jar of wine I sit by the flowering trees,
I drink alone, and where are my friends?
Ah! the moon above looks down on us,
I call and lift my cup to his brightness.

Prohibition has shorn this country of her dignity and the dignity of her citizens as well. Great men wanting a drink would have to sneak about to get it. After it is obtained, it cannot be sipped in comfort. I believe that wine is as necessary to life as literature, music and art. To prohibit wine would be to deprive the world of many fine poems and pictures. Wine is the natural heritage of Mother Earth.

> *If Heaven loved not wine*
> *A wine star would not be in Heaven.*
> *If earth loved not wine*
> *The wine spring would not be on earth.*
> *Since heaven and earth loved the wine,*
> *Need a tippling mortal be ashamed?*
> *The transparent wine, I hear,*
> *Has the soothing virtue of a sage—*

But the drinker here must forever be on the lookout for a possible raid.

If the people want prohibition, I think it should be on cars. People here are becoming slaves to the automobile. Young men have not gone to work very long before they are drawn into debt by an attractive Ford or Nash in some show window. And before long, they will have killed somebody, if not themselves. Thus the indemnity coupled with the unpaid installments would take them a year or two to pay. When all those are paid, the car will have become out of style, and a new one is needed. And so the vicious circle repeats itself.

Another thing which ought to be prohibited is candy. Although sweet, it makes people sour. Besides, ladies get fat eating it, a very deplorable condition.

Farewell.

MY DEAR FU:

Our life in the Bamboo Valley in China seems very romantic and out of the ordinary to the people here. To us

47

in China, drinking and making merry are natural, but here in the Occident, poets must do something else besides merely writing poetry. They must either make tours lecturing to people who do not know or understand poetry, but who pretend to live on it, or sit in a classroom teaching young people who see no use in your telling them about the mad raving (in the student's opinion) of men dead and gone long ago.

Farewell.

DEAR FU:

Yesterday a kind benefactor took me to the University of Hawaii. To this institution, boys and girls go to study. They sit side by side and learn from the same books. I wonder how the boys can stand having the girls watch them suffer ignominious failures in their courses. I would never tolerate it. It would lower their opinion of our sex as a whole, which is not as it should be.

It is very interesting to watch how the class is conducted, the girls' physical education class for example. Some girls take it at 7:45 in the morning. This class is either swimming or tennis playing. Before the class, the girls have 15 minutes for changing into gym clothes. Supposing it was tennis playing, they play for fifteen minutes and then the remaining 15 minutes is left to dress. What they gain from the 15 minutes of playing is lost in the hurry and bustle of dressing to be on time for the next class.

Another seemingly useless class is the zoology laboratory. There the most insignificant things are placed under the microscope and studied. Animals of whose existence we were better off if we were unaware of them, are minutely dissected and their every detail studied. Notice the queer kidney of the ascidian. "Do you see it?" "No, I don't, but it should be there." "How many blood vessels has that rat?" "I don't know, my specimen is abnormal, so it cannot be depended upon." Girls who should only be dancing and singing and whose hands should hold nothing more bloody than a flower handle dead rats as if they were pets.

Do you remember my poem which was inspired by Lady Yang Kuai Fei?

She is the flowering branch of a peony
Richly laden with honey dew.
Hers is the charm of the vanished fairy,
That broke the heart of the dreaming king.
In the legend of the Wind and Rain,
None could be likened unto her
Save the Lady Flying Swallow
Newly dressed in all her loveliness.

Can you imagine these women zoologists inspiring me to write such a poem?

Well, with "prohibition" and "feminism" in the air, I don't think I will remain here very long. So you can expect me back in China any day.

Your humble servant,
LI PO.

The Submission of Rose Moy   Li Ling-Ai

Characters

Rose Moy: A Hawaiian-born Chinese college girl who is
Western in ideas and ideals—and yet not
entirely Western. She wishes to become a
leader in China on woman suffrage.

Wing Moy: Her father—a Chinese aristocrat of the old
school who is thoroughly Oriental in his ideas
concerning a woman's place in this world. His
relationship to his daughter is that of a
typical Chinese gentleman—a mere
acquaintance. He thinks that he will insure
her future happiness by marrying her off well.
He interprets a woman's happiness as home,
children, serving her lord, submission—an
interpretation of Old China. Hawaii has never
influenced him.

Kwang Wei: A rich old Chinese merchant of Honolulu
who possesses three concubines in China. His
first wife has died and he is out looking for a
young modern Chinese girl to take her place.
She is to be a creature on whom he would be
able to lavish his wealth, but he also expects
her to be submissive.

Len Donald: A thoroughly American artist who in his
contact with Rose Moy, who has been sitting
for him as a model for a Chinese painting,
as learned of her ambitions, and is helping
her in every way to study things that are
American and to break away from old
Chinese traditions concerning a woman's
place in the world. His relation to her is that
of a teacher and pupil.

Servant:	A young man in the service of Wing Moy.
Scene:	Living room of the Wing Moy residence furnished in typical Chinese fashion—rows of teakwood chairs on each side, ancestor tablets with incense in front. Two tables in the center of the room against the back wall which is hung with tapestries. Two doors on right and one on left at back. The tablets are between the doors.
Time:	Early in the morning.

————

(Wing Moy is receiving Kwang Wei as a visitor. Kwang Wei has come to ask for the hand of Rose Moy. They are seated on the right of the stage.)

Wing Moy: I am honored, my good brother, by your illustrious presence. *(Turning aside and clapping hand to servant)* Tea! *(Motions Kwang Wei to seat. Servant brings tea and sets it on the table.)*

Wing Moy: To your honorable name! *(Lifting teacup)*

Kwang Wei: To your illustrious family! *(Tea ended)*

Wing Moy: What good wind blows you here, my brother, that you honor my humble abode with your august presence?

Kwang Wei: My honorable Wing Moy, I am a businessman in America. Therefore I shall be brief in what I have come to say. Our sage, the illustrious Confucius, says that the basis of a government is the family. Since my first wife, the delicate Po Ling, passed on to the

51

"Kingdom of the Gods," leaving me alone with my concubines with no male issue to continue the Kwang family line—to pray before our ancestral tablets when it is my turn to ascend to the "Kingdom of the Gods,"—I have been most miserably lonely.

Wing Moy: I thank the gracious Buddha for my child, girl that she may be!

Kwang Wei: And I have come to beg of you the hand of your adorable daughter.

Wing Moy: My daughter! But she is young.

Kwang Wei: She will graduate from the University in June.

Wing Moy: Yes, but she knows nothing about the world!

Kwang Wei: *(Disdainfully)* What woman knows anything about the world! I am not asking that your daughter become a sing song girl. I desire her for my wife.

Wing Moy: You have three concubines! My daughter will never consent.

Kwang Wei: You are her father! Why should she consent? Is not a man the head of his own home?

Wing Moy: *(Admonishingly)* You forget that my daughter has been brought up in America.

Kwang Wei: And you forget that she is only a girl. Who will protect her when you go to visit the "World Beyond?" I can offer her silks and satins, and jewels, everything that a woman can care for. Within the four walls of my palatial home, she will lead a calm, peaceful existence, embroidering and singing and raising my men children to perpetuate the great and noble name of Kwang. What more can a woman ask than to live the protected life of her mother, and her mother's mother before her?

Wing Moy: I bow. The law of our ancestors is supreme, my honorable Kwang Wei. (*Hits gong. The servant enters.*) Request the presence of your mistress. Tell her that her father desires to speak to her.

Rose Moy: (*Coming from the right entrance expectantly*) as Mr. Donald arrived yet?

Wing Moy: What! Is Mr. Donald coming again?

Rose Moy: This will be my last sitting for him. The portrait he is painting of me is done with the exception of the finishing touches.

Wing Moy: Hereafter, you will pose for no more artists!

Rose Moy: Pose no more?!

Wing Moy: No more! I sent for you to tell you that tomorrow I announce your betrothal.

Rose Moy: (*Exceedingly shocked*) My betrothal! But I have my college work to finish yet!

Wing Moy: Calm yourself, my daughter. Come bow to the illustrious Kwang Wei, your future husband.

Rose Moy: (*Pleadingly*) Save me, my dear father! You cannot be in your right mind! Mr. Kwang Wei already possesses three concubines in China!

Wing Moy: Yes—the honorable Kwang Wei possesses a great name. Your men children will bear an illustrious name.

Rose Moy: Name! Name! Would you sacrifice your only daughter to be a fourth concubine for a name?

Kwang Wei: *(In a bribing manner)* Think of the comforts and jewels that I can offer you—the pearls, the diamonds, the jades. I would even buy you a Packard roadster, though none of my other wives has ridden in anything but a Ford. *(In a commanding tone)* I shall go to prepare for the betrothal feast. You will make your daughter consent. *(Bows. Exit—through left entrance.)*

Wing Moy: You will lead a protected life if you marry Kwang Wei.

Rose Moy: Yes, my dear father, but what of my college career? Do you forget so soon the promise you made me last year?

Wing Moy: What promise?

Rose Moy: You said that you would let me go to New York to pursue post-graduate work.

Wing Moy: Why must we discuss your life work after graduation now? It is six months from now to June. Be patient, wait till the time comes.

Rose Moy: *(Impatiently)* But I cannot wait. If I am to be the fourth concubine of Mr. Kwang Wei, I would like to know whether I can finish my studies first.

54

Wing Moy: *(In a consoling tone)* We shall discuss the subject in due time.

Rose Moy: In due time which may mean never! *(With determination)* We must decide now! Why must you break into my college career with this betrothal?

Wing Moy: *(Calmly)* You are a girl. You need a man's protection.

Rose Moy: But you forget that I am a modern woman. You forget my ambition to become one of the first Chinese educational women leaders Hawaii has ever produced.

Wing Moy: *(Grandly)* I do not forget. It is a great honor for you to strive for a higher degree, but the risk for attaining such an end is exceedingly great—yes, exceedingly great. You are only a girl.

Rose Moy: Yes, I am a girl. But this is America and we are living in the twentieth century.

Wing Moy: Nevertheless, you are a girl, the daughter of Wing Moy, whose father before him was Kwong Moy the great mandarin of Ning Po. As a daughter of an illustrious house, you will marry as the women of our noble name have done before you. You will marry another eminent house in order that your sons may perpetuate another great name.

Rose Moy: Yes, then we would be continually living in the horrible past. The present and the future—that is what counts in America! If you do not consent—

Wing Moy: Is this what your college education has done to you? Fool that I was to send you to college!

Rose Moy: Yes, my education has taught me to think for myself—to rise above the shackles of tradition that have bound our women from time immemorial, and have imprisoned their spirits.

Wing Moy: And it has taught you to spurn the protection that an illustrious and noble man offers—to break our venerable traditions. *(Shaking his head regrettingly)* Oh, fool that I was to send you to college!

Rose Moy: Then you do not consent to my going to New York for post-graduate work?

Wing Moy: I do not. You will prepare for your betrothal to Mr. Kwang Wei.

Rose Moy: Why must my life be governed by such dusty and diabolical traditions? *(Very indignantly)*

Wing Moy: For centuries, our women have been kept within their courtyards.

Rose Moy: Imprisoned! Bound for a mere existence of slavery!

Wing Moy: But they were happy and content and our home life has run a course as smooth as the breast of the Nuuanu Stream you see yonder—unrumpled by silly whims and fancies. Their supreme desire was to serve their lords.

Rose Moy: Like slaves!

Wing Moy: They bore men children to perpetuate their family line. They were mothers of men.

Rose Moy: And nothing else! Oh father, don't you know that this is an age in which women strive for careers other than that of domestic drudgery? Have you not often praised the Island-born Chinese girl for her initiative in earning her own living by teaching?

Wing Moy: Yes, my rose blossom, but you are the daughter of Wing Moy. Remember your heritage. The women of our family have always been sheltered and treasured. You cannot break a tradition. Your are of the East—you are a Chinese.

Rose Moy: *(With a determined voice)* I can break and I WILL BREAK a tradition when it is an obstacle to my life's ambition.

Wing Moy: *(Quite aggravated)* You cannot break our venerable traditions! You are my daughter!

Rose Moy: I am your daughter, but I will not become tied down against my will to a mere existence with an old man who already has three concubines. Give me liberty, give me freedom—the right of a higher education—and what I desire the most—to lead a worthy career as a great leader of women!

Wing Moy: *(Contradictory tone)* A woman's leader in revolt! *(Commandingly)* I am your father and you are my daughter. I know what is the best plan for your future. I command your marriage to the illustrious Kwang Wei. And verily I say unto you, prepare yourself for the wedding ceremony on the fourth day of the new month! Woe be unto you if you heed not my orders!

Rose Moy: *(Sadly)* You will be sorry.

Wing Moy: Prepare yourself for the betrothal feast tomorrow. Compose yourself within the hour before my return. I go to inform our relatives with the news of your happiness. *(Exit)*

Rose Moy: *(Bitterly)* Ha! My happiness! *(Kneeling before Kwan Yui, which is posed on table on right side of the stage)* They say you have a merciful heart. Help me now, oh Goddess of my mother. *(Rises and looks discouraged)*

Servant: *(Enters)* Mistress, Mr. Donald is here.

Rose Moy: *(Indifferently)* Mr. Donald? Show him in.

Mr. Donald: *(Full of life)* Well, my rose blossom, just one more sitting and we shall have a prize-winning portrait.

Rose Moy: I am sorry Mr. Donald, but I am not in the mood to pose for you.

Mr. Donald: *(Surprised)* Not in the mood?

Rose Moy: No.

Mr. Donald: *(Disdainfully)* Pooh! Surely, there must be some other reason or else you would not disappoint me this way.

Rose Moy: *(Positively)* There is no other reason. I do not want to pose for you today.

Mr. Donald: But this is the last sitting.

Rose Moy: *(With aroused emotions)* And I am not in the mood to look pleasant. *(Sadly and slowly)* Mr. Donald, I am betrothed. Do you know it? Betrothed—I say, betrothed!

Mr. Donald: Betrothed! Why, you ought to be overjoyed!

Rose Moy: *(Bitterly)* Yes, overjoyed when I am to marry Mr. Kwang Wei.

Mr. Donald: *(Very surprised)* What—that old beezer! I am told that he already has three concubines in China!

Rose Moy: It is the will of my father, and his word is law.

Mr. Donald: The will of your father! Good gracious, girl! Will you let a mere thing like that bind you, ruin your career, bring you drudgery and untold woes? Oh, flee dear girl, flee as you would flee from the snare of a demon!

Rose Moy: Oh, I know I am a coward. But I am a girl—and yet—

Mr. Donald: Yes, and yet you are an American college girl.

Rose Moy: *(In a tone of distress)* Oh, if only I had someone to back me up! I have no desire to marry anyone. I want to become a great leader of women someday.

Mr. Donald: *(Suddenly)* I know—and say! I have a plan!

Rose Moy: What is it? Quick!

Mr. Donald: You sure you want it?

Rose Moy: Anything as long as it is not marrying anyone!

Mr. Donald: Well—listen! We are going to fool the old beezer. Meet me tonight at twelve o'clock. I will be waiting under your window.

Rose Moy: How will I know that you will be there?

Mr. Donald: Listen for my whistle. I'll help you catch the Matson boat which sails tomorrow morning for San Francisco.

Rose Moy: But I don't know anyone there.

Mr. Donald: You can live with my sister in Berkeley, work for her and study at the same time.

Rose Moy: I'd go if I were sure—

Mr. Donald: They cannot do anything to you if you are away and independent of them financially. Come, spunk up!

Rose Moy: *(Undecided and yet eager to go)* I wonder—

Mr. Donald: *(In a convincing manner)* Of course you want to go. Think! You surely do not wish to be bound for the rest of your dear life to an asthmatic, crab-figured old man with three concubines. Remember, you want to be a woman leader someday. Remember, you are an American-born Chinese girl.

Rose Moy: Yes, I do honestly want to be a leader someday.

Mr. Donald: Then you must go away to study. Traditions or no traditions, it is imperative that you leave home!

Rose Moy: Wait for me tonight, please. I'll go. *(Mr. Donald leaves.)*

Rose Moy: Yes, I will go! No tradition will fetter me! *(Kneels before ancestral tablets)* Oh, angel mother, help me! Help me, I entreat thee!

(Wing Moy returns from visit. He goes to Rose Moy who is bowing before ancestral tablets. Rose Moy turns to look at him.)

Wing Moy: I have notified all the members of the Moy clan of your coming betrothal. You will prepare for it immediately.

Rose Moy: My dear father, before I go to prepare myself, may I ask you one question?

Wing Moy: Yes, my daughter.

Rose Moy: What would my rose blossom mother say if she were living and knew of my ambitions and your plans for my betrothal?

Wing Moy: *(Thoughtfully)* Your rose blossom mother. *(Goes to ancestral tablets and bows slowly three times. Rises and turns to Rose Moy.)* Your rose blossom mother, before she passed on to the "Kingdom of the Gods," put into my hands a letter which she bid me to give you on your betrothal eve.
(Goes to a treasure box which is on a table on left side of stage, and takes carefully from it a letter in a Chinese envelope of white with a red stripe down center.)

Here is the letter. *(Hands it to Rose Moy who looks at it with an amazed look.)*

Rose Moy: *(In a dreamy sort of a tone)* A letter from my dear little angel mother!

Wing Moy: *(Calmly)* Yes. Read it before the dawn of your betrothal day. I go now to order the delicacies for your betrothal feast. *(Proudly)* Shark fins, and birdnest soup, pickled fish, and roasted duck—such a betrothal feast that the guests whom Wing Moy invites will never forget. *(Exits)*

Rose Moy: *(Slowly)* My rose blossom mother! I shall read your letter—yes, I shall read it but not on my betrothal eve as you would have it, but on the eve of my departure. *(Exits)*

(Incense burning in clouds before ancestral tablets)

(Enter Rose Moy, right entrance carrying a suit case)

Rose Moy: No one comes! Now for freedom! If I stay I will have to become the fourth wife of Kwang Wei. If I go, it will mean uncertainty—but the continuance of my education on the other hand—and mayhap a future leader of the Chinese women. I choose to go, and go I shall.
(Starts to go—when gong strikes twelve times from somewhere back of the stage. Rose Moy pauses, becomes a little excited, looks about her—starts to go again. Then she looks back longingly, makes a startled motion to show that she remembers something.)
(Someone whistles "Yankee Doodle"—back

stage.)
Mr. Donald is waiting!
(Rose Moy takes letter from right side pocket of jacket. Opens it and reads aloud.)
"My Dear Rose Blossom Daughter:

I am leaving you to ascend to the 'Kingdom of the Gods.' I cry out to my ancestors to let me stay longer to care for my little rose blossom daughter, but it is their will that I go to the 'Kingdom of the Gods.' Yes, it is their will and their will is my law.

My little one, someday in your precious life, you will understand what the law of your ancestors means. I pray from a mother's heart that when that day comes, you too will bow to the will of your ancestors. It will be difficult for you, I know, for you are reared in America, but remember—you are a child of the East—you are a Chinese.

Remember the voice of your people's gods. May the gods of our ancestors bless you till eternity.

With tears from a mother's heart,

Your Mother."

Rose Moy: The will of my people! But I want freedom! *(Slowly but with determination)* I want freedom! *(Looking at ancestral tablet)* Little angel mother, I cannot—I cannot stay! My urgent duty calls me thither! *(shaking her head)*—I cannot—I cannot stay!
(Someone whistles "Yankee Doodle" outside. Mr. Donald is still waiting.)
(Rose Moy starts to go, then looks back again. The incense rises up in clouds before the ancestral tablets. A gong sounds solemnly and slowly somewhere outside.)

(Rose Moy walks slowly and sadly to ancestral tablets and kneels.)

Rose Moy: *(In a trembling voice)* Oh, gods of my ancestors, to thee I cry! Help me! Help me decide what course I should take!
(She rises, stands pensively for a while, as if listening to a voice somewhere. Then suddenly cries out)
The gods of my ancestors—the law of my people! *(Bows before the ancestral tablets)*
(Slowly and submissively) Yes, my rose blossom mother, I am of the East—I bow. I submit to the will of my ancestors!
(Falls down in a fainting pose before the ancestral tablets. Incense keeps burning.)
(Outside a whistling of "Yankee Doodle" is heard. Mr. Donald is still waiting, and he waits in vain!)

CURTAIN

Ghost Dogs of Halaula   Reuben Tam

Islander, surrounded,
staring over the rim of the channel, living
under schedules of cane fire and roadwork signs,
the vast Pacific taunts you as it flows unbounded,
rhymed to an unremitting horizon and timed only
to the recurrences of the moon.

If only your greenseeded fields could grow forever
into the reaches of your tropical latitudes
the way the plovers of Alaska
bind their north and south into a continuous season.

The hills of the coastal plain where you were born
have been stripped of their alluvial cover, and now
erode down to the reefs where you used to fish.
Coral beds lie under brown silt.
You have seen the broad slopes of Nonou
shrivel through programs of excavation, dying
the mud death of leveling.

Along the road up to Kokee there's a slow illness,
the gashes of last year still bleeding red oxide,
the new blackberry gone mad up and down the ravines,
and the rainforest birds pale as specters in fog.

Tonight. Stars over the island.
Seasons ago white frangipani, jasmine and gardenia
sprinkled the night yards of the sugarcane camp
at Halaula, half a mile upwind.
Listen. Over the abandoned fields you might hear
ghost dogs howling through empty plantation alleys.

The Sand Crab Trap   Reuben Tam

The boy arrives breathless on the shore of the bay
in the first light of morning
to inspect the five-gallon tin trap
he had sunk into the sand the evening before.

The rasp and scratch of claws rise like steam
over the rim of shining metal
as he gloats over his catch of sand crabs.

He will remember this morning in the fractured light
on carapace, the wire legs tangled in frenzy,
the gasping through froth,
the hundred b-b eyes pointed at him,

and all around him the humming of dunes in the sun,
the sparkle of lace-making wave water,
and an east wind too gentle to turn the day,

unlike the wild wind that swept through his sleep
last night,
whipping the steel-thorned vines of bougainvillea
up and down against the wall by his bed,

scratching the runnels of dream,
to drop him
onto a wide white morning laced with salt blood.

Waimea Canyon   Reuben Tam

I was standing at the guardrail
by the canyon rim
when the side of a cliff fell before my eyes.
I had witnessed my island eroding.

But then, if I had been looking the other way
I might have seen a goat nibbling ledge grass,
or a cloud clawing through lehua blossoms,
or the huge island itself
spending its silence.

Land with its flowers and deaths
keeps no appointed time with us.
It heaves under the glitter of streams.
It breaks in a shard of clay.

If I happen to be on a mountain
photographing birds of the rain forest,
or on a plane exquisitely scheduled
between Kauai and the mainland,
it may be that down there, under the layers,
a tremor of my island is rippling the bays
of Peru or Ketchikan.

For You a Lei   Wai Chee Chun Yee

Characters

Mrs. Lee: the mother

Miss Carter: a school teacher

Ah Mui: Mrs. Lee's daughter (about ten years old)

Ah Quon: Mrs. Lee's son (about fourteen years old)

Leilani: a neighbor and Hawaiian friend of Ah Mui
          (about ten years old)

Scene: A portion of a quadrangle enclosure
          surrounded by tenement buildings in the Aala
          Park district of Honolulu. The action takes
          place at the back of a tenement dwelling on a
          projection jutting out from the tall building
          and used as a porch and general playground
          for the children as well as a laundry room. A
          clothes line with a few pairs of faded sailor
          mokus and garments made of flour bags
          flapping in the wind is stretched across stage
          right from a tall pole to the back wall of the
          flat. An ironing board and a laundry tub are
          standing at stage right. A dilapidated railing
          surrounds the so-called porch.

          Upstage left and center are seen in the near
          distance, the backs of rickety tenement
          buildings silhouetted against the pale blue
          sky. A few garbage cans hanging out crudely
          below the windows and flapping clothes lines
          relieve the sameness of the tall gray
          structures.
          At the rise of the curtain Ah Mui and Leilani

are stringing purple bougainvillea blossoms into leis at downstage left. Both are seated on the floor.

———

Leilani:	How long da lei now?
Ah Mui:	Ah-h, short yet.
Leilani:	Ah Mui, you slow wahine. Me mo' fast dan you yet.
Ah Mui:	Yah? You t'ink so only.
Leilani:	Suah, you wan start mo' first dan me.
Ah Mui:	Wal, why you no start first den?
Leilani:	You t'ink me seesy? Everyt'ing gotta start mo'first dan everybody?
Ah Mui:	Suah. *(pause)* Ah-h, Leilani, you waste-time-kine bugga.
Leilani:	Waste time yerself.
Ah Mui:	Aw, shat ap.
Leilani:	Shat ap, yerself.
Ah Mui:	C'mon. No make noise. By'm by da baby goin' wake up and my modda goin' make me carry 'im, you know.
Leilani:	Why? Your ole lady goin' come home today?
Ah Mui:	She wan come home already.
Leilani:	Oh, I though she only come home Sunday.
Ah Mui:	Nah, da boss wan tal her come home, 'cause

tomorrow lei day. Da boss goo-ood you know. Da boss let her come home spacial days, too.

Leilani: Gee! da lucky, boy!

Ah Mui: Yah, but she gotta go back and take care da boss baby tomorrow and stay dere.

Leilani: Ah-h, waste time den, dat kind job.

Ah Mui: Yah, dat's what we tal her, but she no like queet. She say if she no take da job she gotta work night time cannery anyway. So she rather have goo-ood boss and mo' dong-dong and no come home night time.

Leilani: Gee, but my ole lady got one mo' batter job dan dat. She only gotta work day time, and every night she bring poi home. *(Sneeringly)* Your ole lady no bring not'ing home night time, huh?

Ah Mui: Nah! I wan tal you she gotta take care da boss's baby and sleep dere. Now you t'ink she goin' bring anyt'ing home?

Leilani: Yeah, da't why my ole lady say da pake wahine next door lolo for make money, boy. Da kind job she got, she mo' batter no work.

Ah Mui: She wan tal dat about my ma?

Leilani: Suah, and she say, waste time wan your old lady come home. She only good for hit your seester, Ah Lan. Everytime we hear Ah Lan yell, boy. We no stink ear, you know.

Ah Mui: Yeah, I know. *(Pause)*

70

Leilani:	Hey, for why she want to give Ah Lan goo-ood lickin' den?
Ah Mui:	For why you want to know, huh?
Leilani:	Naver mind for why.
Ah Mui:	Wal, mind her own beeswax den. And anyway my ma always bring ono t'ings home Sunday, see?
Leilani:	Not so ono as da kind we get. Gee, da ono pipikaula, boy. And she wan tal me I can wear Kaiulani's white dress tomorrow for da lei program.
Ah Mui:	Gee! I wan get one peachy new dress for tomorrow, too.
Leilani:	Yah, show me, show me.
Ah Mui:	Nah, I not goin' show nobody, see?
Leilani:	Yah, you Jew, dat's why.
Ah Mui:	You t'ink me Jew only, but I no care. I no goin' to show nobody, see?
Leilani:	Yah, you scared, dat's why.
Ah Mui:	Who wan say I scared, huh?
Leilani:	I wan say, of course. I bet you no got da dress. *(Pause)* Yah, I t'ink you wan bull, hanh? Sure, you wan bull.
Ah Mui:	I naver.
Leilani:	Yah, I bet you wan bull.

Ah Mui:	*(Louder)* I naver. Cross my heart.
Leilani:	Go 'head, go 'head. Let me see. *(Ah Mui makes the sign of the cross.)* You no crook now.
Ah Mui:	Nah, I no crook.
Leilani:	O.K. You gotta show me da drass by'm by, you know.
Ah Mui:	Maybe. Hey, look. Your lei wan feenish already. Gee, da swal bugga, boy.
Leilani:	Goo-ood, hanh? Gee, I naver know wan pau already. *(Displays the lei proudly)*
Ah Mui:	*(Rising from the ground excitedly)* Try tie 'im, try tie 'im. *(Grabs lei from Leilani)* Gee, da swal, boy.
Leilani:	*(Reaches for the lei, but Ah Mui swings it away from her and hurriedly ties the two ends together)* C'mon, Ah Mui, give me back 'im. *(Starts chasing her)* Hurry up, boy, or I kick yer pants yet.
Ah Mui:	Yah? I like see. *(Starts off into a hula with the lei stretched before her and sings, "For You a Lei" slightly off key)*
Leilani:	C'mon, I no kidding, you know. You like me slap your head down?
Ah Mui:	Suah. You try. *(Darts away)*
	(Leilani finally catches her by her dress and raises her hand as if to slap her, but Ah Mui, in giggles and laughter gives her the lei.)

Leilani:	I bet you wan spoil 'im already. *(Slaps Ah Mui's hands)*
Ah Mui:	*(Slapping her back)* Aw, nuts. You look, same like before.
Leilani:	Yah? You lucky you naver wan spoil 'im, boy. *(She puts it around her neck.)*
Ah Mui:	O-oh, da swal, boy.
Leilani:	Goo-ood, yah? *(Starts off into a rhumba and sings "La Cucaracha" in a loud voice. Ah Mui joins in with the singing and claps the time for her.)*
	(A baby is heard crying offstage, although the children continue unheedingly with their singing and dancing. Mrs. Lee enters from stage right with a large basket of clothing in her hands and a baby struddled across her back. Mrs. Lee is dressed in a two-piece Chinese costume of plain material. Her hair is disheveled, and, as she walks, she drags her ragged slippers along with her. Quite untidy, she is a middle-aged woman of slight build.)
Mrs. Lee:	*(Amidst the baby's wailing)* What's-a-matter you keeds, anyway? I wan tal you no make so much noise.
Ah Mui:	No, not me, not me. *(Mrs. Lee sets basket on the floor.)*
Mrs. Lee:	Yah, I wan hear you, too. Hurry up, carry da baby. I gotta iron clothes. *(She unties the strap around her shoulders with Leilani's help and sets the baby on Ah Mui's back. The baby stops crying.)*

Leilani:	Ah Mui, we go feenish da lei?
Ah Mui:	O.K. You make dis end, and I make da oder. *(They both take the same position as in the opening of the scene.)*
Mrs. Lee:	*(Picking up basket of clothes from the floor, walks toward the ironing board. Turns on the heat and shakes out a wrinkled child's dress and dips her fingers into a bowl of water set on the board. She wets the clothing.)* Ah Mui, where Ah Lan and Ah Hong?
Ah Mui:	Dey wan go peeck flowers by Aala Park.
Leilani:	Yah, near da river.
Mrs. Lee:	Why go tal 'em go peeck some mo' flowers? You feenish da lei already.
Ah Mui:	Yah, but no 'nough flowers for dis one. *(Shows the half-finished lei.)*
Mrs. Lee:	No make so long den, if no 'nough flowers.
Ah Mui:	Goofy kind if short.
Mrs. Lee:	Everyt'ing you say goofy kind. Mo' batter you no wear lei.
Ah Mui:	Yah? Da teacher say everybody gotta wear lei tomorrow.
Leilani:	Yah, and we goin' have program...
Mrs. Lee:	Ah Mui, you go tal da teacher only reech-kine peepul wear long lei all right...long kind, short kind, any-kind all right. Poor peeepul go hana-hana, O.K. If no get flowers, no

wear, see?

Leilani:	But we goin' have program, see? My ole lady goin' let me wear Kaiulani's white dress tomorrow.
Mrs. Lee:	Yah? Wal, Ah Mui goin' wear dis one, see? *(Lifts up an old, faded blue dress.)* Dis one all same white, huh?
Leilani:	Where her new dress for tomorrow?
Mrs. Lee:	No mo' new dress.
Leilani:	You naver wan get Ah Mui one peachy new dress?
Mrs. Lee:	Nah, no mo' dong-dong for buy clothes. You t'ink every day get new dress?
Leilani:	*(To Ah Mui)* Hah! You wan cross your heart honest-to-goodness you get one peach new dress. Ah-h, you beeg crook!
Mrs. Lee:	Ah Mui, you wan tal lie, huh? You t'ink you funny? I slap your mouth yet.
Ah Mui:	*(Carefully changing the subject)* Ma, da baby wan sleep already. Take...
Mrs. Lee:	You wan tal lie or no, huh?
Ah Mui:	*(In a frightened voice)* Ma, da baby wan sleep already.
Mrs. Lee:	You damned liar. Just like da oder keeds...For why you go school anyway. For why, huh? Only good for learn how tal lie.

Ah Mui:	*(Stamping her foot)* Ma, I wan say da baby sleep already.
Mrs. Lee:	Wal, go put 'im in da bed. What's-a-matter wit' you? You dumbbell! *(Slams the iron down with a bang. Ah Mui goes quickly offstage with the baby.)* All da keeds just da same. Only know how kaukau planty, tal lies and dumbbell.
Leilani:	*(Meekly)* Ah Lan not so dumbbell. Wan you no stay home, she take care goo-ood da baby, Ah Mui, Ah Hong, and Ah Quon.
Mrs. Lee:	Yah, take care! Nuts! She only good for go out and no stay home. Just like now, wan I come home she no stay. Who wan tal her go, anyway?
Leilani:	Ah Mui wan tal her go, 'cause she no mo' not'ing to do.
Mrs. Lee:	Yah, no mo' not'ing to do. Get planty clothes iron, get planty clothes wash. She good for not'ing.
Leilani:	Yah, but now she get somet'ing to do. She go peeck flowers.
Mrs. Lee:	And maybe she goin' fall inside da reever wit' Ah Hong, huh?
Leilani:	Gee, maybe. *(Pause)* If she fall inside da reever by Aala Park, you no mo' lei, Ah Hong no mo' lei, and Ah Quon no mo' lei.
Mrs. Lee:	For why, me no mo' lei?
Leilani:	You know for why? Because if she fall inside

da reever she no can make lei for you, too.

(Ah Mui reenters.)

Ah Mui: Shat ap, Leilani. No tattle. Ah Lan goin' give you good lickin', boy.

Mrs. Lee: What Ah Lan tal you, Leilani?

Leilani: Ah-h, Ah Mui no like me tal.

Mrs. Lee: Naver mind Ah Mui. You tal me.

Leilani: Wal...*(Looks questioningly up at Ah Mui.)*

Ah Mui: I no care. Up to you. I'm not goin' get good lickin'.

Mrs. Lee: No listen Ah Mui. She pupule jest like her seester.

Leilani: Wal, Ah Lan wan say she goin' make one lei for you, because you come home today, and she like hoomalimali you, because...

Ah Mui: Shat ap, she goin' lick you, you know.

Leilani: Because...

Ah Mui: No blame me now, when you get black and blue.

Leilani: Because she wan play hooky today.

Mrs. Lee: Hoomalimali me, huh? Everytime go play hooky and da teacher come scold me. Wan she come home I goin' hoomalimali her...yah, wit' one bamboo.

Ah Mui:	See? I wan tal you no say not'ing.
Leilani:	No tal her I want tal you now.
Mrs. Lee:	Hmph, she t'ink she can fool me, huh?
Leilani:	No, she naver wan say dat. She only say...
Ah Mui:	Ma, somebody coming up da steps.
Mrs. Lee:	Yah? Who dat? Ah Lan? *(Puts down the iron)*
Ah Mui:	*(Turning toward stage left)* Nah, one haole wahine.
Mrs. Lee:	Da one who before bring rent money?
Ah Mui:	Nah, not da one. *(Leilani also looks toward stage left.)*

(Miss Carter enters from stage left. She is a young school teacher of medium height and about 25 years of age. She is simply dressed in a sports outfit.)

Miss Carter:	Hello, girls, is your mother at home? *(Ah Mui and Leilani giggle.)* Isn't your mamma Mrs. Lee?

(Ah Mui and Leilani giggle again.)

Ah Mui:	Yah, she over dere. *(Points at her mother)*
Miss Carter:	Oh, yes. *(Going over to Mrs. Lee)* You're Mrs. Lee, Ah Lan's mother, aren't you?
Mrs. Lee:	*(Stopping her ironing)* Yah, I Mrs. Lee.
Miss Carter:	I'm Miss Carter, Ah Lan's teacher. Kalakaua

Junior High School teacher. *(Ah Mui and Leilani step up to Miss Carter and eye her curiously.)*

Mrs. Lee: Yah, Ah Lan go Kalakaua Junior High. *(Resumes her ironing. Ah Mui and Leilani are in giggles again.)*

Miss Carter: Are these little girls Ah Lan's sisters?

Mrs. Lee: Yah, Ah Mui, Ah Lan seester. Leilani, Ah Mui friend. *(Pause)* Ah Mui, go breeng one chair out for da teacher.

Ah Mui: O.K. *(To Leilani)* You hol' 'im. *(Handing lei over to her)*

Miss Carter: Oh, I don't want to make you keep your friend waiting. *(Ah Mui exits stage right.)*

Mrs. Lee: Nah, dass all right. Leilani no care.

Miss Carter: Mrs. Lee, is Ah Lan at home now?

Mrs. Lee: Nah, no home. She go peeck flower by Aala Park, for make lei.

Miss Carter: Oh, yes, tomorrow is lei day. Ah Lan has been picking flowers all day?

Mrs. Lee: Me, I don't know. I go hana-hana every day...only today, after lunch time, boss tal me come home all right. *(Ah Mui reenters with a chair. Miss Carter sits down and thanks Ah Mui.)* Maybe, Ah Mui know.

Miss Carter: Ah Mui, has Ah Lan been picking flowers all day?

Ah Mui: Nah, after school wan peeck only.

Leilani: Yah, morning time she wan go movies wit' her boy fran.

(*Ah Mui makes a dash for Leilani, and both begin to slap each other.*)

Ah Mui: You look out, boy.

Leilani: Yah?

Ah Mui: Suah, wait for wan she catch you, boy.

Mrs. Lee: (*Snapping a dress at them as they run before her*) Shat ap, you keeds. (*A baby is heard crying offstage again.*) You wan wake up da baby already. (*Pause*) Ah Mui, go carry da baby go Aala Park play.

Ah Mui: (*With relief*) O.K., O.K., Yah, we go, Leilani, we go?

(*They both exit stage right.*)

Miss Carter: Mrs. Lee, I came to see you about Ah Lan.

Mrs. Lee: Yah?

Miss Carter: You see, Ah Lan doesn't come to school every day, and we wanted you to know.

Mrs. Lee: Ah Lan play hooky! No go school?

Miss Carter: Yes, she play hooky. Sometimes she comes to school and says that you make her stay home to do house work and to take care of the baby. Is that right?
(*Ah Mui and Leilani reenter from stage right*

with the baby straddled on Ah Mui's back.)

Mrs. Lee: Ah Mui, you go tal Ah Lan come home queek.
And tal her take Ah Hong home, too.

Ah Mui: O.K. *(She and Leilani go offstage at stage left.)*

Mrs. Lee: *(To Miss Carter)* No, I no tal Ah Lan stay
home take care baby. I tal her go school. Next
door wahine take care until Ah Lan pau
school. She only clean house and cook for da
keeds.

Miss Carter: Oh, I see. But, she says she has to take care
of the house when you're not at home.

Mrs. Lee: Yah, me no stop night time. Gotta hana-hana
for kaukau. Take care boss baby night time.

Miss Carter: But doesn't your husband go to work?
(Pause) Hana-hana?

Mrs. Lee: No, no got husband. Husband muckee.

Miss Carter: Oh, I'm sorry. Then you come home only once
a week from hana-hana?

Mrs. Lee: Yah, me no can help.

Miss Carter: I don't want to meddle into your business,
but we like Ah Lan in school. She's a good
girl, and learns fast, but she doesn't come to
school every day.

Mrs. Lee: Yah, by'm by she come home, I lick her.
Everytime she play hooky, I lick her.

Miss Carter: Yes, she tells us you whip her many times.
No, we don't want you to do that. *(Pause)*

81

Mrs. Lee, do you think you can get job for
only day time hana-hana?

Mrs. Lee: No, no can get. No 'nough pay for five fellas.
Big boy only sell newspaper get money. No
mo' rent money pretty soon.

Miss Carter: ...because if you have day hana-hana, Ah Lan
can have time for homework, for study. Then
you can sleep every night at home.

Mrs. Lee: Me, I try, but no can. Ah Lan bad girl,
anyway. Dat's why she play hooky. I geeve
her dong-dong for buy t'ings for baby and
keeds kaukau, but she use dong-dong for
moving peecture. Dat's why I geeve her good
lickin'. Yah, den she goin' get one mo' good
lickin' for play hooky today.

Miss Carter: But, Mrs. Lee, Ah Lan is a young girl yet. She
doesn't understand.

Mrs. Lee: Yah? Me, I wan come Hawaii from China wan
only fifteen year old. Me, I marry ole man,
get keed, go hana-hana. Why Ah Lan no can?

Miss Carter: But, Mrs. Lee, we want Ah Lan to come back
to school every day and not only a few days.
Principal says this time is the last time Ah Lan
can play hooky. He's going to report to
police. You don't want that do you?

Mrs. Lee: Me, I no can help. Ah Lan I tal go school I
lick her. She no go school I lick some more.

Miss Carter: Well, we can put her in the reform school for
girls, if you don't want to help Ah Lan. You
want that?

Mrs. Lee: Me, I don' know. Maybe yah, maybe no. You mean I geeve dong-dong for put in school?

Miss Carter: No, you don't have to pay. This school is only for girls who steal and play hooky. Bad girls go there.

Mrs. Lee: Yah, me likee. Too much good. Ah Lan bad girl.

Miss Carter: You don't want to put Ah Lan in reform school, do you?

Mrs. Lee: What dat? Refawm, huh?

Miss Carter: School for bad girls.

Mrs. Lee: Suah, good. Ah Lan put inside all right. Maybe pau one year she good girl, huh?

Miss Carter: But, you don't have to put her in the reform school, if she goes back to regular school tomorrow.

Mrs. Lee: Yah, but Ah Lan no like go school. P'oho dong-dong. Every time play hooky. *(A siren is heard offstage.)*

Miss Carter: Don't you think you can help her by getting hana-hana during the day? Then she doesn't have to be staying at home with the children at night herself?

Mrs. Lee: Nah, she no stay home. She go moving peecture. But me no can help. Put inside school all right.

Miss Carter: Mrs. Lee, Ah Lan works hard, but she doesn't come to school every day. Please don't put her in the reform school.

Mrs. Lee: Yah, but goo-ood put inside refawm. Mrs. Wong get her keed inside too. No need lick'em, no need kaukau money. Not'ing. Yah, put Ah Lan inside all right.

Miss Carter: Well, if you really want to, I suppose there's nothing I can do.

Mrs. Lee: Pretty soon Ah Lan come home. I tal Ah Mui go tal her come home. You like her go refawm now? Now all right?

Miss Carter: No, I'm not putting Ah Lan in reform school, but I want her to come back to regular school tomorrow, so that principal will not report to police. Ah Lan is not a bad girl. She's a good girl.

Mrs. Lee: Nah, she bad girl. You tal principal I like Ah Lan for go refawm.

Miss Carter: Are you sure you want to do that?

Mrs. Lee: Yah, me suah.

Miss Carter: Then I'll...(*Ah Quon enters from stage left whistling. He is dressed in a work shirt that hangs loosely at the sides, and in a pair of faded sailor mokus. An old shoe box is strapped across his shoulders. He is barefooted.*) Oh, is this your big boy? (*Ah Quon stops his whistling suddenly.*)

Mrs. Lee: Yah, dat Ah Quon. (*Tossing head toward Miss Carter*) Dat Miss Carter, Ah Lan teacher.

Ah Quon: Oh, you Miss Carter?

Miss Carter: Yes, I am.

Ah Quon: Ah Lan told me about you. She said you help her all the time.

Miss Carter: Oh, but we all are glad to help Ah Lan in school. She is a very fine girl. *(Ah Quon shifts his weight from one foot to another and twists his neck in great embarrassment. He finally sets his shoe box in a corner.)* I was just telling your mother that we are anxious to have Ah Lan in school again. If you can get her to come back tomorrow, it would be wonderful, because we're having a lei program, and I'm sure that she would like that.

Ah Quon: All right I tell her by'm by.

Miss Carter: Oh, would you? That will be fine. *(Getting up from her seat)* Well, Mrs. Lee, you try to see what you can do for Ah Lan. We really would like to see her in school again.

Mrs. Lee: O.K., O.K.

Miss Carter: Good-by.

Ah Quon &
Mrs. Lee: Good-by. *(Miss Carter exits stage left.)*

Ah Quon: Ma, what da teacher tell you?

Mrs. Lee: She wan say Ah Lan play hooky again. Da principal like put her in refawm school if she no go back tomorrow.

Ah Quon: And what you say?

Mrs. Lee: I say, O.K. Put Ah Lan inside.

85

Ah Quon: Ma, you crazy wahine. Dat's calaboose, you know.

Mrs. Lee: Calaboose?

Ah Quon: Sure. Da teacher naver told you?

Mrs. Lee: Suah, she wan say school for bad wahines. Wahine who play hooky and jabone.

Ah Quon: Well, what you like Ah Lan in dere for?

Mrs. Lee: Wal, Ah Lan make me seeck, see? Everytime I gotta lick her. Everytime I come home, da house stink, and da baby no got not'ing for eat. Waste time dat kind wahine, so I goin' put her inside refawm school.

Ah Quon: Yeah, in calaboose. Dat school make her worser. Where's Ah Lan now?

Mrs. Lee: She wan go peeck flower Aala Park. I wan tal Ah Mui go tal her come home, but I t'ink she no listen to nobody.

Ah Quon: Hey, ma, if I tell Ah Lan go back to school tomorrow, how much you goin' give me? (*As he is playing with knife on floor*)

Mrs. Lee: Not'in!

Ah Quon: You know, I think she like go, only she scared you wild beast. Every time you give her good lickin', so she don't want to go when you tell her.

Mrs. Lee: O.K. Tal her go back if you like. Tal her anyt'ing. I no care.

86

Ah Quon:	If I tell her, you give me two bits? Huh, ma?
Mrs. Lee:	Nah.
Ah Quon:	Ah-h, you Jew bugga.
Mrs. Lee:	Nah, no mo' two bits. *(She stops ironing and turns to gather clothes from line.)*
Ah Quon:	Wal, twenty sants den.
Mrs. Lee:	Nah, no mo'.
Ah Quon:	Sure you get. You only Jew.
Mrs. Lee:	*(Throwing clothes gathered from line into basket and sitting down on chair)* Twenty sants for tal Ah Lan for go back school? Nuts!
Ah Quon:	Dime, den.
Mrs. Lee:	You pupule. Scram out. *(Pause)*
Ah Quon:	*(Sighing)* Den I gotta tell her for not'in. But I gotta geeve her somethin goo-ood, or else I t'ink she no go back, boy.
Mrs. Lee:	I geeve her good lickin' an' she still no go school. What you t'ink you goin' geeve her?
Ah Quon:	Dat's what I askin' you. I don' know. *(Pause. He gazes at the lei on the floor.)* Oh, ma, for who da lei?
Mrs. Lee:	Me, I don' know. For Leilani I t'ink.
Ah Quon:	Ah, ma! I t'ink I know what I goin' geeve Ah Lan for go back school tomorrow. One lei!
Mrs. Lee:	You look out, boy. Leilani goin' keel you if you

jabone her lei, boy.

Ah Quon: What you t'ink? I not goin' jabone her lei for geeve Ah Lan.

Mrs. Lee: What you goin' do? Make one?

Ah Quon: Nah! I goin' buy one peenk carnation lei for her. Yah! One peenk carnation lei. Sure t'ing she goin' back for da lei program, boy. Yah, den she no got to go reform school. Yah!

Mrs. Lee: You one mo' pupule guy in da house, or what?

Ah Quon: Sure, I pupule. I goin' buy one peenk carnation lei for Ah Lan go school tomorrow and tal her, "for you one lei." Yah! "For you one lei." Sur t'ing she go, boy. Yah! *(He rubs the palms of his hands together quickly and whistles the tune of "For You a Lei" and exits with his shoe box strapped around his shoulder.)*

CURTAIN

These Unsaid Things   Charlotte Lum

Characters

Pa: A man in his late fifties. His sparse hair is
            beginning to turn grey at the temples. He
            owns a small business but isn't much of a
            success at it. He is tyrannical and has a little
            of the artistic temper.

Ma: His wife is very practical. She is rather
            stockily built. She has greyed much more
            than he. She loves her children but doesn't
            know how to show it.

Lin: One of the children, about 23 years old. She
            is quite plain. She has the kind of face that is
            not quite used to smiling and laughing. She
            appreciates some of the same things her
            father does but there is no common ground
            because a barrier of silence has been built
            between them. She, like her parents, seem
            indifferent to members of the family, but
            doesn't mean to be.

Father: the inner self of Pa.

Mother: the inner self of Ma.

Daughter: the inner self of Lin.

Notes: The latter three characters speak more slowly,
            and in a lower tone of voice than their
            external selves. They do not always fight their
            external selves because they have been so
            long suppressed by them. The inner and
            external selves of one person speak freely to
            each other. The inner selves of all three

persons speak freely to each other pleasantly, affectionately, and kindly. The inner self of a person can speak to the external selves of the other two, but the external selves of these two cannot hear or speak to him. The external selves snap, bark, snarl, and shout at each other. Father, Mother, and Daughter move about with Pa, Ma, and Lin respectively with an economy of motion. They each stand behind their external selves.

Attire: Pa has on a pair of brown trousers and a long-sleeved tan sports shirt. Father wears a faded pair of khakis and a thin white shirt.

Ma wears a teal blue Chinese gown and Mother wears a light grey one.

Lin has on an emerald green dress of severe cut, designed to cover as much of her femininity as the light green dress of softer lines brings out in the Daughter.

The facial features should be minimized with make-up of a cold color.

Scene: The living room of a low-middle class Chinese home in Honolulu. In a prominent place are hung two big photographs side by side. These are probably photos of some relatives two generations back. There is a rocking chair with several unfinished trousers DR on the right side of the doorway, a sewing machine UR to the right side of the rocking chair, a table UR against the upstage wall, cluttered with blocks of wood and tools, and a round table with nine stools around it, DL. There are partially carved figurines on the table UR. A screen door UC opens into a dark hallway. On the wall left of the round

90

table are shelves; books on the top and wooden figurines on the bottom. There is a built-in desk below these shelves. A nest of teakwood tables on the L of the UC doorway holds a telephone. Reed chairs are put in appropriate places.

———

It is early afternoon on Saturday. Pa and Ma are seated at the round table, he on her right two stools apart. Ma has her back somewhat to the built-in desk. He is reading the morning paper while eating, she is peering down through her bi-focals and carefully picking over food with her chopsticks. They eat in silence for a while. She looks around the table at the empty places, looks at him and heaves a sigh, then resumes picking.

Ma: (*snapping at him*) Stop your reading and eat, Pa.

           (*he has his eyes on the paper*)

Mother: (*more pleasantly*) Please eat your lunch Pa. (*Pause*) No, you can't hear me, Pa, can you. Ma won't let me talk to you the way I want to.

Father: (*not unkind, smiling a little*) This dish is tasteless.

Pa: (*sharply*) Have we got any parsley?

Ma: Yes, we have some.

Mother: Please get it yourself this time. I'm tired. I don't want to get up, Pa.

Father:	You used to be so nice about getting things for me, Ma. Please, do get some for me.
Pa:	(*stopping his chopsticks in mid air and looking at her. She continues to nibble.*) Well, get some!
Ma:	(*slamming her chopsticks on the table and getting up*) Someday, old man, no one's going to wait on you. Then what'll you do, old man?
Mother:	Go get some, Ma. He'll like you the better for it, even though he won't say it. He really must be nice, Ma, inside him—as much as he is mean outside.
Pa:	Get the parsley! (*Ma stands, arms akimbo, glares at him, emits a loud "humph!" and exits L. Pa continues to eat and read.*)
Father:	She seemed tired, Pa. You should have talked more kindly to her. But you hardly ever listen to me. You're always hiding me behind you. (*Pa takes the top of a chopstick and digs into his ear, trying to scrape something out. He turns in the direction of the kitchen door.*)
Pa:	What's taking you so long, woman? (*Pa's eyes sweep proudly over the wooden figurines on the shelf.*)
Father:	Beautiful pieces of wood carving, Pa. (*Pa's eyes stop at a particular space. He strains his eyes, gets up and walks to the shelves and picks up from the floor below the shelves a*

figure that had been knocked down.)

Pa: Sonnabitch! Ma, who knocked Ching Li down? The arm's broken.

(Ma re-enters with parsley)

Gän-fän!* Why can't people be more careful? How could it be knocked down from up there? *(puts broken figure and part on desk)* Who—
(*Corruption of "confound," pronounced gan fan.)

Ma: I don't know and if I knew I wouldn't say. Enough talking. Finish your lunch.

Mother: Tommy was tossing his ball around here this morning, Pa. He's only a little boy. He doesn't know how much these things mean to you, Pa.

(Ma and Pa settle down again)

Father: Where are our children, Mother? 'Way past noon and only two of us at lunch.

Mother: They'll come home soon, father.

Ma: What time, Pa? *(no answer. She taps his newspaper with the tops of her chopsticks.)* What time?

Pa: *(stops reading long enough to look at his watch and without looking up at her, says)* Twelve-forty-five.

Mother: She's late for lunch. Call her, Ma. If you don't the poor thing will probably go without eating. Call her.

Ma: *(calls to someone UC)* Lin, come eat. Stop your packing and come eat.

Pa: *(drops his paper)* Packing? Where is she going?

Father: What have we done to her?

Ma: *(sighs)* She came home from the university about an hour ago and said she was leaving.

Pa: Why?

Ma: I didn't press her. I think she'll tell in time.

Mother: I wanted to know why, but you wouldn't let me find out. She's a strange one to you. I know her. She's not happy here. Please, won't you let me talk to her, Ma?

Pa: Why couldn't you find out? You're her own mother.

Father: I don't blame you, Ma. You were anxious but you don't know how to talk to her. Twenty-three years, twenty-three years with us but we hardly know her, mother. She's getting farther and farther away from us.

Ma: *(snapping at him)* And aren't you her father, too?

Mother: I shouldn't be so hard on you, Pa. You really think a lot of me and the children, don't you? Don't be afraid to show them that you care— don't.

Pa:	(*trying to squirm out of this*) Well, it's *your* duty as a mother to find out.
Father:	I've been telling you all the time, Pa, that it's our duty too. You wouldn't let me talk to her the way you know I should.
Ma:	If you'd done your duty as a father all along—
Mother:	Well, Ma, have *you* done yours?
Pa:	(*riled at being driven out in the open*) Pighead! You unreasonable sow! You—
	(*Ma doesn't move an eyelash. It's a familiar arc in this vicious circle. Lin enters with Daughter from UC. As soon as she steps in, her shoulders seem to drop a little lower, her steps drag a little heavier, and her face becomes less animated.*)
Ma:	(*filling rice bowl*) Come eat.
Lin:	Yeah, in a minute. (*Lin crosses toward kitchen, stops, goes to table to see what is on it.*)
Mother:	Please eat, Lin. Please eat something.
	(*Pa had stopped abruptly on seeing her enter. He resumes reading.*)
Lin:	Oh, *that* again.
Daughter:	I'm not a bit hungry, Mother, but I'll have some. I'll sit with you two for the last time. (*Lin turns to go, stops at Pa's speech*)
Pa:	People should learn to eat what's put before

them.

Father: Don't let Pa frighten you, my daughter. Please sit down and eat.

(Lin turns to stare at Pa)

Daughter: I'm not afraid of you, Pa. I'm not afraid any more of your ranting. It's just that you and I don't feel comfortable within sight of each other.

(Lin exits into kitchen. Daughter remains on stage)

Father: A man doesn't have any comfort in his own home with an indifferent child in it!

Pa: Tell her to bring the tea.

Ma: *(staring daggers at him)* Bring the tea!

Pa: *(clacks his tongue loudly and tries to swallow)* Hah—why you always put so much salt in fish? Makes a man's guts shrivel up inside him.

Father: This sauce is very good, though.

Ma: If it's too salty, don't eat it. A saltier fish goes a longer way.

Mother: I know it's salty. I'll remember next time.

Pa: Salt fish is salt fish. But fresh fish should have a taste all its own.

Father: You're not much of a cook, Ma, but your dumplings are delicious.

Ma: Look, next time we have fresh fish, *you* cook it.

Pa: But woman! After 27 years of cooking, don't you know—

(Lin re-enters with tea and a tall glass of ice water. She coughs conspicuously. He stops abruptly. He picks up the newspaper and scans the articles.)

Father: Say something. Say something, my daughter, don't look so—not that way—so cold, so harsh.

(Pa straightens the paper and looks around for the Chinese newspaper.)

Pa: *(pointing to side table under wall shelves)* Get me the Chinese paper behind you.

(Ma turns around in her chair and reaches for the paper. She throws it down on the stool on Pa's left.)

Father: Thank you, Ma.

(He picks it up, lays it on the top of the one he's just read)

Mother: You're a smart man, Pa. Not many Chinese men nowadays can read both English and Chinese.

(Lin has by now put the tea on the left of Ma who handed it over to Pa on her right. She sits on Ma's left.)

Daughter: *(to Lin who is busy nibbling)* Pa's smart in many ways, but too bad, he doesn't know how to be a really likeable person.

(Pa pours himself some tea. Ma gets up and crosses to the rocking chair. She starts working on her sewing. Lin picks up chopsticks and tastes the fish.)

Lin: *(addressing no one in particular but directed at Pa)* I think the fish is just right.

(Lin sits down and puts back half the rice Ma has served her.)

Mother: Oh, Lin, I should have guessed you couldn't eat much now.

Daughter: The fish *is* salty.

(Lin takes a sip of water and begins to eat.)

Pa: *(rustling his paper)* It says here old man Mau Ting died.

Father: Where are you going, Lin? Why? You sit there eating so calmly.

Daughter: You're wondering too, Ma, where and why I'm going, aren't you?

Ma: Mau Ting? Who is old man Mau Ting?

Mother: *(pleadingly)* Lin, please tell me where you're going. I want to know.

Daughter: Don't feel badly about me, mother. I can take care of myself.

Pa: He's George Mau's uncle.

Father:	What do I care about Mau Ting or George Mau? *(Pause)* What are you thinking about, Lin?
Daughter:	Your words are only to fill in the dreadful emptiness of silence, Pa.
Ma:	Oh, yes. That filthy rich merchant—how old was he?
Pa:	He was sixty-five, that sly fox.
Ma:	His daughter-in-law's a lazy one.
Mother:	But Ma, she has three sons and you have only one.
Pa:	She's a beautiful woman.
Daughter:	You shouldn't have said that to Ma.
Father:	Yes, you shouldn't have, Pa. That must have hurt her.
Ma:	*(tauntingly)* Hmm-mm, so the old man still notices beautiful women.
Mother:	Yes, I know I'm not half as good-looking as she.
Daughter:	And why shouldn't anyone look on a thing of beauty?
Pa:	Why shouldn't I? There is little enough in life to give one pleasure.
Father:	She's a beauty but she hasn't half a brain in her pretty head.

Ma:	There is plenty enough to keep one busy at earning a livelihood.
Mother:	Ma, you're jealous. It's showing.
Pa:	Woman, you don't understand these things!
Father:	Ma's jealous—it seems then, she does care, Pa.
Ma:	A woman like her should have other more important things to be doing—than, than, flirting with greying old men.
Mother:	What else is a beautiful woman to do, Ma?
Pa:	You think up the insanest ideas. She's never flirted with me or anyone that I know of. She's respectably married and what's more, she has three sons—that's more than you can boast!
Father:	You should have bitten your tongue on that last, Pa.
Ma:	Old man, if *I* had anything to say about bearing male or female children—
Lin:	*(putting down bowl and chopsticks)* Pete's sake! Why do you always have to argue? Can't a person eat in peace?
	(Lin stands up and looks around for something. She sees the morning paper under Pa's Chinese paper. She makes obvious efforts to look around for something. During this business:)
Father:	I don't blame you, Lin. Why shouldn't you get angry?

Mother:	I'm sorry you have to listen to the same thing every day, Lin. I thought you're used to this by now, Lin.
Daughter:	But I'm *not*. I can't stay here any longer. I must go—somewhere—anywhere—But wait, you must tell them, Lin.
Lin:	*(addressing no one in particular but directed at Pa)* Where's the morning paper? *(without looking, Pa lays it on the stool next to him. She picks it up and sits down again.)*
Father:	You can't even speak directly to me. I'm an ogre in your eyes, isn't that so, Lin?
Mother:	Why don't you try to be civil to him, my daughter? It won't hurt to try—it won't hurt for all of us to be nice to each other.
Daughter:	Why do I keep doing things like that? I should have asked you directly for the paper, Pa. You wouldn't quite know what to do if I did, though, would you, Pa. I'll spare you the discomfort. *(Pa goes UR to the work table and picks up some unfinished work)*
Father:	If Pa had a chance to do it over again, Lin, maybe we'd be talking to each other the way we should. *(Pa pulls up a low bench and sits on it. He begins to carve, letting the shavings drop on the floor.)*
Ma:	Stop that, you old goat! You're dirtying the

floor again.

Mother: Let him do it, Ma, he usually sweeps it clean afterwards.

Pa: *(looking at the floor around him and grunting)* Well, it isn't any too clean!

Father: Don't get her angry again, Pa.

Ma: Go and find some old newspapers to catch the shavings. You'll have us all living in a pig pen soon.

Mother: Get it for him, Ma. A man doesn't like to be ordered about.

Pa: Look, old woman, I'm not asking you to sweep up after me.

(Ma gets up from rocker, crosses to desk and finds some old newspapers.)

Father: Better use it, Pa.

(Ma throws a small batch of newspapers at his feet with a loud thump.)

Ma: Here, now, use it, you old goat!

(Ma returns to her rocker, plops in it and continues to sew.)

Pa: *(protesting while spreading the newspapers on the floor)* But I've got some on the floor already!

Father: Do it, Pa. Here you sit grumbling while Lin over there is troubled, trying to find a chance to talk to you and Ma.

Lin: It says here that the price of beef is going to be eight cents higher by the end of this year.

Daughter: What is the matter with us? This is my last day here. They're anxious to know why I'm going.

Ma: Hah—it's like eating gold itself.

Mother: You poor thing, you don't care about *that* now. You've got other things to worry about.

Daughter: Here you sit and talk about the price of beef, Lin, when you have to tell them why you're going—tell them. Tell them now.

Lin: *(clearing throat)* It says here that rice in China now costs 16,000 Chinese dollars a bag.

Father: What a pretense, Lin. That doesn't mean a thing to you, but it's good to hear you talk.

Ma: Better to die than work that hard for a few grains.

Daughter: You're not listening to what I'm saying, Ma.

Pa: Chinese dollars! Chinese dollars aren't the same as American dollars. How stupid can a woman be?

Father: You're worried, Ma, you're not listening.

Ma: Perhaps not as stupid as a good-for-nothing husband. Keep out of this.

Mother:	Ma, you know you didn't mean that—about his being—
	(While external characters speak, inner selves try to restrain them with gestures, with half audible sounds)
Pa:	*(voice rising)* Good-for-nothing, am I? Old woman, watch your tongue!
Ma:	Yes, a good-for nothing—even a dog won't want you for a master!
Pa:	You dull-witted woman! You're not worth the spit to argue with!
Ma:	Don't spit out your filthy saliva here, pig!
Pa:	A she-devil if ever I saw one! When I—
Lin:	Oh, stop it! Stop it! Stop it, I say! *(they cower slightly)* One can't say anything here without having it picked to pieces! You fight like cat and dog. Other people have fathers and mothers. It seems our parents are untamed beasts!
	(Pa and Ma busy themselves with their work.)
Daughter:	Oh someone should strike me dead for saying that. Why must we always growl at each other? Pa's always starting it. You're sensitive enough to want to defend yourself, Ma. But it doesn't sound nice. You *want* to be nice to each other just as much as I do, but we don't know how or we don't dare. Why are we afraid to? I should say 'I'm sorry', but I can't. I *feel* sorry for having said that but when I say it out loud, the words are empty. Oh, Ma, I'm awfully sorry. I'm

sorry for having said that to you too, Pa.

Father: Go, Lin, wherever you're going. Try to find peace for yourself.

Mother: Go, Lin, wherever you're going. Try to find some rest.

(Lin stands up.)

Lin: You want me to clear the table, Ma?

Ma: Leave the food on. Cover it.

(Lin gathers the used utensils and takes them into the kitchen.)

Daughter: Do you like saying things like that to each other, mother? Do you father? If you don't say things like that, there isn't anything else to talk about, is that it?

(Lin re-enters with a clean white dish towel to cover the food.)

Father: Those things we say, Daughter, do sound terrible. We shouldn't snarl at each other that way.

Mother: We shouldn't be taking it out on you and the children.

(Lin goes over to the book shelves to sort out the books she intends to take with her.)

Daughter: I ought to explain why I'm leaving. Why does it have to be so painful to discuss anything with you two?

Lin:	I'm going to take some of these books with me, Ma.
Father:	Take them? Where?
Ma:	Where are you—I mean, what about your mail? If people ask for you—
Lin:	You're nosey too. But I guess I gotta tell you. I don't know the address, but I'll send it as soon as I get there. I'm going to live in Manoa.
Ma:	Oh, so this place isn't good enough for you?
Mother:	Why? Why do you have to go?
Father:	Why did you wait so long to tell us that, my daughter? We might have made adjustments.
Lin:	I've been thinking of moving for a long time. I can't study here.
Daughter:	*(anticipating Ma's next speech)* Yes I know you made the children double up—that was sweet of you, but I can't stand all this fighting—I can't study.
Ma:	We made the children double up so you could have a room to yourself.
Mother:	You're tired of living with us, aren't you, Lin.
Father:	We're not very pleasant to live with, are we?
Lin:	So much noise here—I mean, people always fighting next door and their radios turned on so loud.

Daughter:	The people next door aren't any worse than we are. Why do we always have to fight and be cruel to each other?
Ma:	Who are these people—where you're going?
Lin:	An old couple. I'll be working for my room and board there.
Ma:	You don't have to work like that.
Mother:	You have to stay away and keep busy so you won't think about being unhappy.
Father:	You keep busy at your studying, but you don't seem happy, Lin.
Lin:	It's near the university. I'll save a lot more time that way. I don't have to waste time riding the buses.
Ma:	But you've been going from here to the university for two years now.
Father:	All these years, Mother, we've been turning our own daughter out of our house. It's too late now. We've lost her.
Lin:	I haven't been doing as good work as I wanted to and if I'm going to spend so much time and money for a college education, I may as well do it right.
	(All three become absorbed again in their own business. A moment of uncomfortable silence)
Pa:	*(clearing throat)* Where are the children?
Ma:	*(shrugging shoulders)* I don't know! One

here, one there, I don't know!

Mother: They're smart. They're out most of the time
to get away from this dreadful house.

Pa: You're home day in and day out, don't you
know where they go or what they do?

Father: And shouldn't *you* know too, Pa.

Ma: That's not easy when one has to work at
these trousers to earn a few extra dollars.
Now if you had more business sense—

Pa: It's not easy in these days of strikes and
unrest.

Father: A business man's life is such a distasteful
one—cheating, pulling strings with some—
kowtowing to others—a man's not his real
self in that kind of world.

Mother: Don't say what you're about to, Ma.

Ma: If you wouldn't spend so much time on these—
wooden—these useless wooden monstrosities,
you wouldn't blame the strikes.

Father: Don't start something again, Pa.

Pa: So that's what you think about my work! I
can almost believe that you deliberately
knocked Ching Li down. If I—

(*Lin takes a book and slams it on the table.
Pa hears it and controls himself. He goes
back to his carving.*)

Father: A man can't do what he wants to in his

own house.

Mother: You must stay. Don't leave Lin. Stay and keep us from clawing each other up.

Daughter: *(with book in hand, examines figures after turning around to see that he isn't looking)* These *are* beautifully carved. What'd happen if I told him so? His blood pressure would rise because I'd said something he never expected to hear. Then, I won't way it. I'll be of more comfort if I didn't. It's too late for saying nice things to each other now.

(Lin picks up a book.)

Of course I'll need to take this dictionary.

(Lin takes the books she has selected toward UC. She stops before she reaches the doorway and reaches for the telephone. She dials.)

Father: Well, old man, she's unnerved you. Stop and have a cigarette.
(Pa does)

Lin: Hello, please send a taxi to 917 Kelly Street. Yes, right away. Thank you.

(Lin exits UC. Daughter lingers long enough to hear the following speech before she exits UC)

Mother: Lin, oh, my daughter, don't go, don't leave now. I want you here. Stay—

Father: Mother, don't keep her. It'd be better for her if she goes.

(Pa goes to a cleared space on the right side

of the round table, puts down the figure he
has been working on, goes to the shelves to
get other figures.)

Mother: Ma, you and Pa aren't good for her.

(Pa puts the other figures on the table too so
as to form a complete train of travellers. He
is not satisfied with it. He brings the broken
Ching Li and places it with loving care among
the others. He picks it up again, picks the
broken part up and tries to fit it in place.)

Father: She's headstrong, Mother. At least we can
            say a decent goodbye to her.

Pa: Gän-fän! Where's the glue?

Ma: Look before you ask!

Mother: It'll be better if Lin left quietly—no tears,
            Ma, no tears.

(Pa glares at her, then goes UR to table and
looks. He opens and slams drawers vigorously.
He picks up a small block of wood to look
under it and throws it down hard,
punctuating it with a loud "Sonnabitch!" He
walks to the sewing machine and looks
through the drawers, finds the tube of glue
and then walks menacingly toward Ma who
looks at him out of the corner of her eye.)

Pa: You knew all the time where it was! All the
            time you're doing things like that!

Father: But, Pa, maybe it wasn't Ma.

(Lin enters UC with two suitcases and a

raincoat)

Ma: I don't know how that got there.

Mother: Pa, you're being unreasonable.

Pa: It couldn't have walked there, stupid!

Father: Pa, hold your temper.

Ma: But I—

Mother: Oh, stop, Ma, what's the use!

Pa: Keep out of my things!

           (Lin puts bags down)

Lin: I used it. I didn't—

Pa: Damn! Damn you! Keep outa my things!
           It's just as well you're going. A man can't do
           what he wants to. A man can't be what he
           wants to be in his own home!

Daughter: You needn't be angry over a little thing like
           this, Pa.

Lin: You don't think I'd stay here another day,
           do you? It's a wonder Ma tolerated you this
           long! Sure, I'm going now.

Ma: *(weakly)* Pa, Lin, keep your voices down.

Father: You're not really angry over this little thing,
           Pa. She's unnerved you—going away like this.

Pa: Go! Go and make yourself a servant up in
           Manoa. Go! I don't give a damn!

Lin:	Stop it! Stop it! I'd rather be that than be a part of your daily cat and dog fights. When I leave, at least I can decide what I want to do with myself. Why do you make yourself so hateful?
Father:	I've really turned her against me.
Pa:	Hateful, am I? This is what you think—what you've thought all these years! You ungrateful child!
Ma:	*(feebly)* Don't—don't fight—Pa—Lin—
Daughter:	Don't say it, Lin. You'll regret saying it.
Lin:	*(with irony)* My dear, loving father—should *I* be grateful?—the times you whipped us—leather belts at that—eating juicy steaks while we kids watched you hungrily—dry bread in hand—the time you slapped Ma when she was pregnant with Tommy.
Pa:	Get out of here!
Mother:	Pa, don't send your daughter out that way!
Lin:	I don't forget things like that! And now, all this constant fighting sickens me. I'm going. I'm glad for this chance. I'm going. Someday, Ma and the kids will be going. Then what'll you do, old man?
Pa:	*(shouting)* Get out! You and everything you have—get out!
Ma:	Stop your shouting, Pa!
Father:	Don't Pa. Don't say anymore. You don't

really want to send her away like this.

Lin: I won't bother you anymore—I'm going—
(*with sarcasm*) I'm going, Lord and master!
(*She bows deeply from her waist to mock
him.*)

(*Lin exits, leaving door ajar. Daughter is at
the door. Ma leans back on her chair, takes
her glasses off and wipes them, puts them
on again. She takes them off again, and
wipes her eyes, then goes back to her
sewing, her shoulders shaking. Pa carves
even more vigorously.*)

Father: She's gone now, mother. She's been getting
ready to go for years now.

Mother: We've been driving her out all these years,
father. We've driven her out.

Daughter: I'm sorry it had to happen, mother—
father. I'm really sorry. I didn't want to
leave this way. I had hoped that you would
say a civil goodbye. Goodbye, mother,
goodbye, father. Be kinder to each other.

(*Daughter exits*)

CURTAIN

Tom Chang's Family History

Tom Chang

March 11, 1977

Dear Family:

I would like to set down a bit of our family history. Popo continues to be hale and hearty, but she is going on her second half of seventy years old, and this may be a propitious time to help my nieces and nephews appreciate her crucial role in bridging her own past, immigrant, minority generation and that of her children who, to me, have stepped into the Western twentieth century society very effectively.

Our first ancestor in Hawaii was Chang Hu (April 26, 1847-1882). We don't know when our great, great grandfather arrived in Hawaii, but it was probably between 1865 and 1873. 1865 is the date of the first large scale immigration of Chinese laborers to Hawaii from Kwan Tung Province. You will note a little later on that he definitely was in Hawaii by 1873. This means that Chang Hu was one of the first group of Chinese coolies in Hawaii. He was probably a laborer who had signed a three-year indentured worker contract with some plantation at $3 per month; one of the thousands of young Chinese men who hoped to make a fortune in the Sandalwood Mountains and return to his native village. He had left a wife in their village (Oo Shak Village in Kwan Tung Province). They were childless, having lost a son who was four years old when he died.

It seems that Chang Hu had relatives in Hawaii, like an older sister. Beyond this we only know he took a Hawaiian wife. He married her formally, and to do this, Chang Hu had to renounce his Chinese citizenship and become a subject of the Hawaiian Kingdom. Consequently all children of this union were Hawaiian subjects, and later, U.S. citizens, a very important fact in the shaping of our own future histories. Chang Hu was never to return to

China. To this day I don't know anything else of his Hawaiian family except he had at least one son, Chang Wun, our great grandfather (May 7, 1876-December 16, 1895). Chang Wun was taken back to Oo Shak to be raised by his stepmother, but the exact details of this event are not certain. One story has it that he was taken back when he was about age four. In any case the child was probably taken to China with the consent of both parents. I am sure Chang Hu would have wanted one of his descendants to have been brought up in the ancestral ways. Possibly the child's Hawaiian mother was also willing to share the child with another woman whom she could feel for, lonely without either spouse or offspring. In any case, you will note that Chang Hu lives for only six years after his son's birth. I wonder how much influence he had on his child. It was Chang Hu's older sister who took the boy back. She was Leong Boo's mother. Remember Leong Boo the jeweler? He is still alive, and once, several years back, I asked him if he remembered any of this; he didn't.

From Chang Hu's dates, you can see that he died a young 35 years old. We don't know a thing of the other members of his Hawaiian family. Story has it that when Goon Goon first arrived in Hawaii, he too was anxious to locate his cousins, etc., but the old Chinese folks discouraged him saying he should leave well enough alone. I myself am very curious to know about the other half of our family tree. There were many Changs from the same village emigrating to Hawaii, so tracing is difficult. (One possible relation may have been the famous police detective Chang Apana—the inspiration for the fictional Charlie Chan. If he is related, he would be distant, though I do remember meeting him once when he conducted the investigation of our home after it had been robbed.)

There is just one other solid piece of information on our great, great grandfather, Chang Hu: his membership in the Chinese society known at Chup Ying Tong (translated: Cultivate English Society) The society was founded on June 30, 1873, by 36 persons with a contribution of $25, and their purposes were largely humanitarian and social. I think the very name they chose was significant and touching. That name is so different from the Black Dragon Society or the Secret Hand Society from other places and other times.

Let us return to our great grandfather, Chang Wun. From his dates you can see that he lived only nineteen years. Though he was half Hawaiian, his values and psychological stance must have been Chinese, having been brought up in China, probably living there from childhood to about 18 years old. Remember he was a Hawaiian subject and therefore might return here anytime, and he did at about age 18, probably. According to Popo, he ran a small store in the Palama area. Chang Wun was not in Hawaii very long, probably a year. Before he left for Hawaii, Chang Wun had married Lum See (December 29, 1876-October 25, 1935), and she was expecting a child. Chang Wun returned to her when their son was about one year old and was home for about eight months when he died in 1895. His son was Chang Kwai, our grandfather, Goon Goon (April 10, 1894-March 22, 1959).

Before closing the chapter on Chang Wun, we can only comment that he died too young to leave much of an imprint. His own father was already deceased when he arrived in Hawaii. The fact that he was able to start a modest business enterprise suggests some financial means, but I doubt he was anywhere wealthy. If his father, Chang Hu, were true to the Chinese ideal, he would have provided his Chinese family back in Oo Shak with at least a modicum of support, and this would be where Chang Wun's nest egg came from. But this money from Hawaii, if it were sent, ended in six years when Chang Hu died in 1882. I suspect that both our great grandfather and our grandfather grew up in poverty and without fathers. It also seems that Chang Wun was of uncertain health. According to Popo, who tells the story probably from Goon Goon, Chang Wun was injured in a fall, and this had a permanent effect on his health.

Goon Goon was just about 20 months old when he

116

lost his father. Subsequently he was raised by two women, his own mother and his paternal grandmother. Remember Chang Hu's Chinese spouse? I suspect the two widows comforted and helped each other and raised their lonely offspring. It was a poverty situation from the stories and the fact that Goon Goon grew up uneducated. He talked about fishing for his supper, doing farming and other kinds of laboring work. He grew to manhood, age 21, in his province and was therefore thoroughly Chinese in mentality and outlook. Remember, he was a U.S. citizen, his father having recorded his birth in Hawaii and had obtained the citizenship papers.

I am sure Goon Goon, as he grew up, knew that he had an escape from this life anytime he decided to take advantage of it. In fact it is a sad story when he finally decided to make the break. He had to trick his mother, lying that he was planning a visit to the port city of Canton, when actually he was planning to ship out from there. Therefore, when he left China, never to return, it was without proper farewells to his mother. I suspect, by that time, his grandmother had died.

There is another tale of narrow escape in his efforts to come to Hawaii. It seems that he had given his citizenship papers to an uncle who turned out to be more sinister than trustworthy. This relative was supposed to take care of the paper work for his coming to Hawaii. But time dragged by and Goon Goon did not hear from him. He finally told another relative about his wait, and this relative upon his arrival in Hawaii checked into the matter and found that the dishonest relative was in the midst of trying to sell the citizenship papers to another person. In any case this was averted and Goon Goon finally arrived in Hawaii in 1915 when he was 21 years old. He was drafted and served as a private in the U.S. Army until World War I ended.

He probably then went to work as a laborer at City Mill Company. He later became a truck driver at the same company. He was employed there until the Depression when he lost his job in about 1932. He was always proud

of the fact that he was a truck driver and that this
required a skill and responsibility not given to many
people. I can believe this because in those days the trucks
were still mechanical monsters and had to be wrestled
with, and I know one of his routes was across the Old Pali
Road, which was more a winding rutted trail than
anything else. Before moving ahead, let us close the past
gently in China noting that Goon Goon's mother gave
birth to her son when she was 18 years old, raised him for
21 years, then lost him, and she lived alone for another 20
years, to die in 1935. But each generation is a bit more
generous than the past one. In her case, she was blessed
to meet her daughter-in-law and grandchildren about a
year before her death, when Popo visited her, bringing
along Uncle Henry, Aunty Anita, and Aunty Ronnie. Popo
was already carrying Aunty Barbara.

This trek to the ancestral home was under very trying
circumstances in the middle of the Depression, and carried
out only at the expense of a heavy loan. The whole event
came to pass only because of spiritual promptings, if we
are to believe Popo. This is an example of the ancestral
spirits that pervade the lives of the Chinese, and if one is
to believe Popo, it was Chang Wun's spirit who
continually urged the family in Hawaii to make this trip
before the old lady died. According to Popo, it seems that
Ronnie had been crying for a couple of days and nights
without clear reason. Popo finally consented to visit a seer,
who said it was simply the cry of the old folks at home
wanting to see the family. It was then that Goon Goon
and Popo scrambled to find the money and make the trip
home. Today we have a photograph of the family on the
President Hoover, which took them home in 1935.

I think it is partly Popo's personally deep religiosity
and her upbringing that has made her talk about these
ancestral presences in such a real way. For example, if one
chats with her at any length, she seems to refer to these
bygone people in a very concrete fashion. They just sound
like friends who are still around. There is nothing fearful
or threatening about them. At the grave, for example,

118

where she sets up her offerings, she talks to Goon Goon just as if they were at the dinner table, telling him about the family and others. I have talked with her friends at the temple and they all employ the same allusions and references.

Goon Goon arrived in Hawaii just about the time the United States went to war and he was drafted into the army in 1915, approximately. As far as I can recall it was a short, intensive experience for him. It seems that he was very fearful that he would die and be buried in some foreign land, forever separated from his kinfolk. Actually his army stint was a beneficial event. It helped him to become a member of his adopted society, giving him an intensive and common experience with others more Westernized than himself. Today his tombstone reads, "Chang Kwai, Private, Headquarters Company, 2nd Hawaiian Infantry, World War I."

Goon Goon and Popo were married in 1921 or 1922. Their first child was born in 1923. They were to have a total of eight children, seven of whom are still living.

He never learned to read or write English and to this day I wonder why. Goon Goon was certainly a bright and ingenious person, learned quickly, was especially mechanical, and yet from his signature, I sometimes suspect that he may have had a reading problem. His signature is tortured and awkward, though he always wrote with a flourish. On the other hand, Popo was well educated in Chinese, so we grew up with Popo taking care of the Chinese language needs, and us kids taking care of the English demands as they occurred.

Regrettably, in the Chinese scheme of things, when a woman marries, she really becomes a part of her husband's story, and her own history is difficult to establish, unless one is to refer to her father's records. For example, when I talked to Popo about these things, she is neither very clear nor very strong about her own family. It is only by close questioning that I am able to piece together many of the details. Her father was Lum Mun Sook. He was an educated man and brought his Chinese wife to Hawaii when he came here, probably about 1890.

All of his children were born here. Popo, Ah Sam, was the third child, and she was in Hawaii until about age four, when her mother took all of the children home with her back to their village named On Tong. Her father owned a Chinese bookstore on Pauahi Street, and it was still there in the Thirties when I as a kid used to hang around there when he babysat us while Goon Goon and Popo shopped. He was also a letter writer, that is, writing letters for illiterate Chinese who wanted to send letters home. I remember listening to him help an inarticulate man compose a family letter by suggesting things to say. He charged them twenty-five cents to fifty cents for a letter. His store was really of pretty good size, certainly as big as the stores in Ala Moana, like Honolulu Book Shop. It was filled with Chinese books and writing utensils, brush pens, ink stands, and other little knick-knacks such stores usually carried. He wasn't a very friendly man, and I never really got to know him.

I am sorry I do not have Popo's birthdate. She was born about 1900, travelling to China when she was about 4 years old and returning when she was about 20. She was an American citizen by virtue of being born in the then Territory of Hawaii. Some of her sisters who were born here and returned to China eventually emigrated to such far-off places as Puerto Rico and Canada. I know Popo is well-read but I do not know just what kind of an education she had in China. She enjoys her Chinese stories and can handle the Chinese almanac very efficiently. She reads the Book of Tao regularly as a prayer.

Anyway it appears she married soon after returning to Hawaii. How she came to marry Goon Goon, how they met, and so on, I am not clear. We all know their life was a long economic struggle with painful as well as happy memories. I think a comment from one of her intimate friends at the temple, Mrs. Young, is fitting. She ran the temple fronting the Nuuanu Stream on River Street and said of Popo that Goon Goon was fortunate to have married a good woman. Together they raised a family who

120

brought them honor and pride. This was what she said, and I know it sounds a bit flowery. But when she said it, in Chinese, looking at me, with those eyes that see right through you, I knew she meant it.

With much affection,

Your Uncle, Tom Chang

Scenes from Childhood: Palolo Valley

Joseph S.M.J. Chang

Chapter One

By the time she said it, it was very late and we had already had a lot to drink. We're not all drinkers in our family, just some of us. It seemed like this was the drinking contingent, or a good part of it.

"Joe, you gotta write my story. You have to write the book."

"Oh, Anita. I don't know if I can."

I let my eyes run past her stare, intent but not too fixed, as though allowing me some room to move, nor yet about to let me free. The table was cluttered with the dishes and bottles and beer cans of the night's festivities.

Although Anita and I are brother and sister, we lived in different worlds.

Mine was a childhood of irresponsible innocence. I was the last of eight children born to my parents. A sister died early, but for me, as you would expect, it is as though she had never taken a breath of air. As I speak to my friends who ask about my childhood in Hawaii, I usually answer that I grew like a weed, basically ignored and untended. Not in the sense of one emotionally deprived; it's just that I was allowed pretty much to grow without too much supervision.

It seemed like my father and brothers could do everything. The world they lived in was full of tools and machines, and to this day, it is a thing of wonder to me that none of us ever became an engineer of any sort at all. And yet Tom did attain status as Machinist, First Class, and Francis was, in effect, a master rebuilder of naval warships, and Henry, as a dentist, is noted for his meticulous craftsmanship.

Barbara lived for the most part with me, in the children's world. By the time we were there, presumably it was only the two of us who were children. Anita and

Ronnie were adolescents, and perhaps more to the point, they were females, and so like females throughout the world and certainly in a Chinese household, they were quickly absorbed into homemaking.

With seven children, the cycle was endless. Clothes to be washed, starched, dried, then sprinkled and finally ironed. Mounds of clothes and endless racks of shirts and blouses, pants and dresses. And because we all went to Catholic schools, the boys wore dress shirts and ties, the girls wore an actual cotton middy, and everything had to be starched and ironed. On Saturday mornings, you could listen to "Let's Pretend," and on Sunday night, there would be KGMB's "Amateur Hour," which was always exciting just because it had real people on it.

The principal job for the women was food preparation, but of course. Just as it only appeared that the men were always pouring concrete or mixing oil-based paints or building things, in memory, my mother and older sisters were always in the kitchen slicing vegetables or plucking chickens or the most tedious of all jobs, removing the foreign matter from the soaking bird's nest soup ingredients.

After the pork had been chopped into a fine hash or the boned filet of fish had been blended by hand into a smooth cake, after all the slicing and soaking of dried mushrooms and red dates and the peeling of the ginkgo nuts, there would then be the wrapping of the won ton or the rolling of oysters in the thin, transparent membranes which came from unspeakable places, forming sausage-like morsels to be fried in deep oil. Everything had to be assembled in the most elaborate and delicate packages; it was the farthest remove from a steak on a grill. Fish cake would be stuffed into little cones of tofu, gelatinous rice would enfold fatty pork, and the rice ball would be wrapped in ti leaves to be steamed for hours.

The Hawaiian foods weren't much easier to prepare, either. The poi had to be mixed with water, with both hands plunged deep into the thick, sticky mass. By repeated opening and shutting of the hands, letting the

123

poi ooze between the fingers, eventually it would all be mixed to the right texture and could be served, after cleaning up, for the grey paste often extended almost up to the elbows.

If it sounds like an idyllic world, it wasn't. It was a busy one, with a lot of work to be done, although I confess never really feeling that I myself had any particular role to fill. They did it all; Barbara and I watched and helped in the meaningless and incompetent ways of little children. Our only real job that I can remember was to come home right away after school to build a fire next to the garage. On a large tripod over the fire, there hung a black kettle. This would be the hot water for baths, for washing dishes.

Because our father was a vegetable peddler who operated out of a truck, we always had many apple and orange crates around. These we used for firewood, breaking them apart as we needed more fuel. Of course, the soft pine was also ideal for making things with, for carving things out of, and I did a lot of that, too. But mostly, we burned the boxes. Only once did Barbara and I lose control of the fire, but the garden hose was nearby and the garage was saved.

A spectacular departure from the usual routine was the St. Patrick's Fair. The church was to hold a fair on its school grounds, and it promised to have booths, pony rides, a ferris wheel and a whirligig. It probably was pretty modest, even by the standards of the pre-war era, and compared to the theme parks of the present, but a fly to an eagle. But then, I was only four.

The church and school were two blocks down the street from us, down 7th Avenue past the bungalows just like our own, and then past the public school, Aliiolani, on one side of Waialae Avenue. That's the main street through our part of Honolulu, where the bus lines ran, and for a time, during the Second World War, where I would stand waiting long minutes while long convoys of military vehicles would run past. Sometimes we would see a cannon being towed, or tanks on trailers, but mostly it was trucks with their canvas covers drawn tightly over the arched hoops. Within, on opposed benches sat the young men, all very pale and white, very young, and very serious as they held their rifles before them, barrels pointed up.

The war is a part of the story, but it properly belongs in another place. The fair comes first. Perhaps it was because the fair was held at night, and the lights shone on the giant wheel, of which it was whispered that people had fallen to their deaths from the great height, that there was so much anticipation. Then too, in those days it seems people did not go out at night. In fact, my family never went out at all, except to visit relatives, attend weddings and bury the dead. To be out at night was simply unusual.

For a four year old boy it was, needless to say, exciting in its stimulation of wonder and fear. The crowds of people were frightening, because if you were swept away from your oldest sister's hands, you might never find her again in the darkness. But then, there was the cotton candy, all puffed up and teased out in airy billows, and the wonder of it all: if you could knock the pyramid of milk bottles off the top of the barrel, you'd get a doll. I knew that I certainly didn't have either the eye or arm for such a feat, but I knew for sure somebody would go home with an armful of dolls.

Anita had been given the charge to keep me in tow, and tow she did. Even then, she had an imperious way, doubtless some of it acquired in imitation of our parents, whose accustomed manner was to give peremptory orders. So she hauled me hither and yon, and we did what she thought would be fun or appropriate. Because of her cynical streak, we ignored all the games of chance; she knew that the odds were always against us. We spent our scrip on what offered a definite return—a ride on the ferris wheel, three times around the ring on the pony.

One thing was free, though, and it was the draw for prizes. I had not been aware of it, but everyone held a ticket for the evening's climax when certain prizes were to be given away. It was all obscure in my mind, as we stood in a mass around the steps which led up to the school auditorium. Up at the top of the wide, wooden steps, where later I would have my class pictures taken with my mates, there was Father Andrew holding up a large black and white rabbit. A bunny!

The rabbit was funny looking, with a black patch over one eye. I had never seen a real rabbit before, and he looked bigger than our cat. I thought for sure he could beat our cat in a fight, if it ever came to that. I wanted that rabbit.

After Father Andrew called out the number, Anita checked her ticket, and then mine. All of a sudden, she told me to stay exactly where I was, and that she'd be right back, and she plunged forth into the crowd and made her way up the steps. I couldn't see exactly what was going on, because the priest had come down a few steps and left the reach of my view. Then he was back up at the top of the steps calling out another number, when Anita got back to me and hauled me off.

Her face was hot and flushed, her mouth turned down with a look of disgust and contempt that would be, for the rest of her life, a trademark. She shook her long, black hair as she pulled me along, away from the lights and the crowds. When we were at the front of the church, with the bishop, St. Patrick, facing away from us toward the busy avenue, looking up to the lights rising up from the floor of the long valley before him, she sat me down and told me that they had stolen my rabbit from me.

"How come?"

"They said the prize was supposed to be for a child under seven."

"I'm four."

"I know. I told them it was your ticket. But they didn't believe me." And her eyes blazed.

Whether it was that the war came, and there were no more fairs to be held, or whether our family just never went back, I don't know. It was the last fair I went to, until I grew up and had children of my own to bring to the Fair.

I admire the writers who have a sure grasp of their material, years and dates well fixed. For me, my life is a blur, at best, a montage. Counting back, now, I know that it must have been 1940 when I started kindergarten, and I must have been in the first grade when the Japanese bombed Pearl Harbor. These truths are like the colored tabs one puts on index files; they come long after the facts, for I cannot in truth remember what grade I was in, or how old I was when the bombs fell.

I was walking home from Mass, probably 7:00 Mass, and one could hear, in the distance, muffled explosions. Looking toward the southwest (though in Hawaii, we never used the compass coordinates because the Islands were askew), I could see puffballs in the sky. And that was all. The dull thud of reverberating TNT ten miles away and a few dark clouds was all the evidence I had that a great war had begun.

It exists as a separate memory, though surely it must have been the same day, Sunday, December 7, but I remember the whole family gathered together to listen to the radio in the parlor, in front of the floor-standing RCA Victrola with its lift-top and automatic record player. I cannot remember the broadcast, only the air of anxiety, the sense of fear.

That night, I believe we all slept on the floor together, in the living room. It was important to be gathered in one place. Was it for the reassurance that being clustered together could provide, or was it to expedite our flight, should there be word of an invasion?

The Japanese did not invade, but no one knew that that would be the case. So for much of 1942, we lived with a fear of attack, which the population prepared for by painting all the windows black, so that when the sirens went off, as they occasionally did, we could keep our lights on. In the early months, we really did experience black-outs. The headlamps of cars were likewise painted over, except for a small, T-shaped opening, which would have to suffice for lighting the way.

As we went to school, every child had to carry a gas

mask, and soon bomb shelters began to appear on the playgrounds and in the schoolyards. Across the street, in the little park, for a while there was a huge pile of discarded war material. What it contained, I cannot recall, except for the choice items, spent casings for artillery and small arms. It seemed as though all the boys in the school had his own collection of polished brass casings for 30 and 50 caliber weapons.

Every now and then, going to school or returning, we would stand at the corner of 7th and Waialae and count the trucks rolling by, heading up toward Kaimuki. I never knew where they were going. Now, I suppose it would have been Fort Ruger on the slopes of Diamond Head. Where they were really going was to invade the islands held by the Japanese, in what we now know to have been a long and bloody process.

It never occurred to me then, but as I think about it now, those men sitting in their trucks never looked like the soldiers we say on the movie screen at the Kaimuki Theater. American soldiers going to war in the movies were, until the eve of the invasion, at least, always chattering with noisy camaraderie. Fearful introspection would be reserved for the last moments before the doors of the landing craft would open wide, a ramp thrust forth, and the tanks and men would pour forth into a hail of fire. The war according to Hollywood.

The men we saw were always quiet, as if on the parade ground, at attention, facing straight ahead, but unseeing. Moreover, they looked different. Not only were they all white, but they all had that pallor which in later years one could use to identify a tourist just arriving from the mainland. It was obvious that their skin had precious little exposure to the Hawaiian sun.

One bright Sunday afternoon, there appeared at 3344 Kaau Street a young sailor, gleaming in his white bell bottoms, middy and black tie, his cap rolled up in his right hand. He was smiling, eager, expectant; he was calling on Anita Chang, who, after all, was a very beautiful girl. Over the years, I've never quite forgotten him, because I always

128

fancied that in his mind, he was doing the proper thing, the sort of thing that he would have done back in Watertown, Wisconsin, or Waterbury, Connecticut. You came calling; you introduced yourself to a girl's parents. And you did it with a bright smile on your face.

The trouble was, he wasn't back home. He was in Honolulu, and he was at 3344 Kaau Street.

Like so much else about our life, we just knew that we weren't to invite our friends into our home. Playing with them in the front yard would be alright; the back yard was not a very good idea, but bringing a friend to see the tropical fish in the large, outdoor tank our father had made could be tolerated. Still, the back yard was within that space which properly considered was private. The house itself, then, was sacrosanct.

Among my friends, I could pass freely into the Nagler household, but then she was a single parent, a haole from the mainland with two sons, Buddy and Buster. How she was stranded in the Islands, I couldn't say, and rumor had it that Buster was illegitimate. The important thing was that she came out of a different social climate, and for her, having her sons' friends in the house was normal. So too with the Jenkins family. He was a black man from California, married to a Chinese woman from Maui, Rose. He was clearly college educated, and Rose was at least second-generation, so for them, too, neighborhood children were not considered strangers.

In my parent's eyes, unless you were a relative or Chinese, you were a stranger, and strangers did not enter our house. By the same token, I never entered the homes of my Japanese friends, the Furutas or the Maruyamas, either. Oddly enough, I had no Chinese friends. There just weren't any boys my age around, while there were many Chinese households scattered throughout the neighborhood.

The point is that I early understood that there were two systems of value as far as people were concerned. One set of rules operated within the house, and then, outside, there was another. This was my first experience in what would be a long process, the same process that would entangle the lives of all of us, negotiating the rival claims of the two worlds. For the door would simply not hold against the currents outside.

The sailor standing at the door probably had not the faintest inkling of how intrusive his knock was. Anita was in the bedroom—our house was too small for anyone to have the privacy of his or her bedroom, it was just one of three bedrooms—and she came to see who it was, wearing a colorful robe. Apart from looking like she'd just gotten out of bed, she wore her usual mask, a flat, unexpressive face. When she opened the door and found the bright smile and the sailor's "Hi!" she turned away and closed the door in one silent movement.

Where my parents were when this incident took place, I could not say. If this was like any other Sunday afternoon, I expect my father would have been in the back yard doing something with his hands and my mother would have been in the kitchen. I don't see how either of them could have known that a sailor came to call; it was all over so quickly. So I presume someone must have told; maybe it was me.

All I can remember is Anita curled up on the parlor floor screaming as my father stood above her, leather belt in hand, lashing her. My mother was trying with no success to stop the attack, and all I can accurately recall is the sense of fear, the unmistakable sensation of violence let loose. It is only a tableau that I can present here; it would be pure invention to describe the scene with greater detail.

It is impossible to say with any certainty what my father's motives were, what he thought he was accomplishing. Certainly, if he thought that he was insulating his family from the greater world, he failed, and the beating was for naught. For we would all go out into that world the sailor came from, and probably far beyond anything he himself, in his young life, ever knew.

130

Chapter Two

With seven children in the family, it isn't surprising that we grew up almost in tiers. Barbara and I were more mascots than siblings, and I imagine that Anita and Ronnie relied upon each other, both being females and close in age. What the interior landscape of their lives was actually like, I can only guess, though it did not take long for me to appreciate how courageous all the females were, for theirs was not a favored lot. As for the three elder brothers, I knew them more as uncles than as siblings. When I was a child, they were, I think, men.

Anita and I must have lived in different worlds. I did enjoy my childhood, as she must have hated her own. Part of the radical difference might be explained by the fact that I was unknowing about almost everything concerning my father and mother. For one thing, the external processes of acculturation were already at work for me and Barbara, because both of us knew a lot less Chinese than did our siblings. So our chances to communicate effectively and extensively with our parents were greatly reduced.

The reason we didn't have the tool is easy enough to guess at. Our parents didn't encourage a lot of communication. Our father was not given to talk. Neither was our mother, for that matter. Were they that way, or was it just the cultural tradition? Meals were always eaten in silence, all of us circumscribing the round kitchen table. The Chinese most assuredly know how to cook, but they seem to be indifferent to the niceties of service. Real Chinese waiters are never gracious, and they will pile the food on a table as though it were a challenge: "Don't you dare complain about this dish, because you probably know nothing about this food you are going to eat! You're lucky I brought it to you."

Often I've glimpsed into restaurant kitchens where there would be two or three waiters or cooks hunched over their bowls, looking like nothing so much as vultures, eating in silent absorption with their food. It always brings me back home.

It's as though members of a household were mutually hostage to some conspiracy; we worked together, but there was no effort to enjoy each other's company. No one spoke; not my father, and not my mother.

It was not a tense atmosphere, not that I was aware of. It was just silent. My father would have his teacup of Scotch whisky, and the meal of two or three courses, plus leftovers, would be served. Sometimes, there would be incongruently Western touches, sliced tomatoes served on Manoa lettuce, slathered over with mayonnaise. Sometimes, there were compromises, a pan fried sirloin steak cut up into bite-sized pieces in the Chinese fashion. Whenever we had fish, either steamed or fried in the wok, my father would always claim the head, enjoying the eyes, the brain and the cheeks. It was a taste I never acquired. How could I, when he always had first choice? It is a loss I have managed to live with, however.

The three brothers all married with the blessings of their parents. Henry was married in the States, but Tom and Francis married in Honolulu, and both had the standard receptions. Their marriages were all a credit to my parents. They had all chosen Chinese for their wives, and this was appropriate. Anita and Ronnie violated the standard. Bill is Filipino, and Tosh is Japanese.

In contrast to my brothers, Anita and Ronnie both eloped. Barbara did not marry immediately, but she too had to strike out on her own, without sanction. Not long after completing her degree, Barbara resigned her job as a grammar school teacher to find employment in Garden City, Long Island. She has been in New York ever since. Where my brothers formally and with approval entered the world of adults, my sisters had to plot their escapes. Obviously, they were entering mutually different worlds, as far as symbols go, for presumably my parents thought that their sons were going to raise Chinese families adhering to the old traditions and values. By their actions, the daughters were not. They were abandoning the past.

Ronnie and Toshio had been going together for a

while, and since they were at the University of Hawaii together with Bill and Anita, the four of them were closely knit. As the kid brother, I was naturally welcome in their midst, and one of the grand experiences of my life was to practice driving around those cane fields on the dirt roads. I can't remember who's Model A it was, but it was wonderful. We'd go bouncing around in that old, rumble-seated roadster, top down, and I'd practice coordinating feet and hands, clutch and gear shift, on those back roads. It was fun and such a relief from the lessons my poor brother Francis felt constrained to offer.

Francis had the first new car in the family, I believe. It was a 1946 Chevrolet two-door fastback. And I was supposed to learn how to drive on his own exquisitely maintained machine. I don't know why he did it; noblesse oblige, I guess. I doubt that he was so instructed by my father; he was probably just doing what had to be done. But it was an excruciating experience, one of the most dreaded of my life.

It was the total sense of incompetence that characterized those sessions behind the wheel. The mask of Job's patience in fact betrayed the conclusion that I was hopeless. I would never be able to make the transition from being braked and in neutral to having the gear engaged and ready to proceed, on a steep hill. Of course it was an essential skill, since the problem represented an actual driving situation, when at a stop sign on a steep hill, with a car behind. You'd have to get going again without rolling back into the car behind.

Francis is a man who admires skill, aplomb and style. He never merely wanted the job done, it had to be done with elan. For Francis, the process of releasing the clutch halfway, to the point where it would engage the motor enough to hold the car, while simultaneously sliding the brake foot to the gas pedal and depressing it so that there would be sufficient torque to hold the car, was a matter of athletic skill. One had to develop the feel for the clutch and the accelerator, and the three movements had to be performed instantaneously. That's where it became poetry.

Obviously, long before one masters this automotive lyric, the car will either roll back, the engine will die, or the car will lurch forward in spasmodic hiccups. Not even prose.

Through every misadventure, Francis would suffer. Even if he didn't move, you knew he was suffering. Even if you were driving in a straight line, keeping pace with the flow of traffic, you still knew he was suffering, because somehow your style was wrong. If I swung too far around a parked car, he might draw on his reserves of hyperbole and say,

"Did you think it was going to jump out at you? Just pass the car; don't go around the block."

When I next passed a parked car and tried to do with greater nonchalance, he'd wince and slide down into his seat, saying,

"If you want to hit a car, why don't you just plow right into it?"

I wanted to learn how to drive, but the price was great. Later, when I would practice driving with Bill and Toshi, I found out that there were better ways of teaching automobile driving. Regretfully, even though I remembered when I was teaching my own children, I knew that I was still doing to them some of the things Francis had done with me. I here publicly apologize to my kids.

Chapter Three

Except for Francis, we all left the Islands, at least for a time, usually to get a degree or two, before returning to finish our lives someplace. One wonders about the drives which were at work. In my short view, I can think about the front page of the *Star-Bulletin*, which, every evening, had a map locating the day's news about the progress of the war. I remember being a Boy Scout, trying to master the manual, to win my merit badges to move up the ladder to First Class, then, Star, then Eagle. I never got past Second Class Scout.

When I think about those Eagle Scouts, in Hawaii, I

am astonished by what they managed to do. *The Boy Scout Manual* was a compendium of knowledge about the natural world; I think its premise was that the good scout, who was always prepared, could survive in that world with little more than a canteen and the four-bladed scout knife. So there we were, assiduously trying to learn the distinctive paw marks left by bears, wolves, possum and deer. The silhouettes of the martin, the owl, the eagle and the robin, in flight and perched on a branch, were there. The distinctive outlines of the oak leaf, the maple, the linden and the elm were also presented to our imagination.

It was all an exercise in the imagination, because it was so remote a world. It never occurred to anyone that the manual was irrelevant to boys growing up in the South Pacific. I wonder if Hawaiian Boy Scouts are still comparing paw prints of raccoon and squirrels. The irrelevance was only a waste of a little time; the more subtle and greater damage was to reinforce the notion that the real world, the world of consequence, was out there on the North American continent.

Chapter Four

Before I began school, some time around the period when St. Patrick's had its Fair, my father took me along with him when he went to work. He always was off early in the morning, before the sun rose.

The first thing he did was to back his truck up among all the others on River Street, which ran along the Nuuanu Stream. This was where all the wholesalers were, and I remember being taken by the hand up that street, where my father would buy the produce he needed to supplement his stock of canned goods and candies. And as he walked up River Street, I was amazed by how many men greeted him, said hello, shook his hand, and his face was sweet with smiles I had never seen at home. He was a man completely different from the man at home.

My father walked up and down the street with a

greeting for everyone, full of confidence and self-assurance. It isn't that he wasn't that way at home; it's just that I never saw him among his peers, as a man among men, rather than a father among his children. He made me feel proud of him; he seemed to know everyone, and what was better, everyone seemed to like him, very much.

The street was busy with the bustle of all these men, peddlers like my father. Their trucks were all variations on the same theme. Our father's truck was typical. It was like a pick-up truck with the difference that it had a roof over it. The sides were open, as was the back, which had the standard drop-leaf gate. In the middle of the truck-bed, there was a row of boxes displaying various canned goods and candies, things like Campbell's soups and Spam, Mounds and Hershey bars. Leaning at an angle in front of the canned goods and candies were the fresh vegetables and produce, oranges and apples, some pineapples, carrots, tomatoes, Manoa lettuce, string beans and the like. The other side of the truck was arranged similarly. At the back, there were buckets of flowers, asters, gladioluses, carnations, gardenias and anthuriums.

When he was driving along, the produce would be protected by canvas attached to the roof secured at the bottom. When he pulled over at one of his stops, where his customers expected him to arrive at approximately the same time every day, the canvas would be propped up and away, forming an awning to provide some shelter from the sun. At the back of the truck, an arm would be swung out for the hanging scale, and he would be ready for business.

River Street was quite a sight, then, with all those trucks lines up, backed up against the curb, ready to accept their wares. On the other side of the walk, the wholesalers, with their boxes and bins. The atmosphere was not much different from what can be found in any American city early in the morning where produce is wholesaled, where there is a lot of dirt, scattered pieces of lettuce leaf or carrot tops, with boxes of spoiled fruit attracting flies, and empty crates piled haphazardly in alleys. The men all wear dirty aprons, and they talk loudly, asserting themselves to the listening world. I can never pass such streets without remembering River Street, on the banks of the Nuuanu. They are places for men, and my father seemed comfortable on his street.

The route took him through the civilian quarters for soldiers and sailors based on the island. I can't say with any certainty where we went, probably around Pearl Harbor, since that isn't far from the city. Maybe he went up into Aiea Heights overlooking the Harbor, but I doubt that we went as far as the Schofield Barracks. Years later, after I returned from California it would amaze me to see how many military installations there were on that island, ranging from the almost plush Fort DeRussy on Waikiki Beach, to the very business-like world of Pearl Harbor.

The customers called my father "John," which surprised me. How that came to be, I cannot guess. His name was Chang Koon Kwai, and he usually signed it as Chang Kwai. I always thought it was a good name, perhaps influenced by the consonant cluster, which closely echoes words and names in the Hawaiian language. It was a name which fit both worlds, the Chinese and the Hawaiian.

I remember a photograph one of his customers made. He stood with a blonde child wearing a cellophane hula-skirt and little bra. He had his wide-brimmed straw hat on, and he smiled broadly at the camera. It that picture, his Hawaiian heritage is unmistakable, asserting itself in his flared nostrils and full mouth. I often wondered what his customers thought of him. I was curious what the maker of that photo, presumably a mother, said when she sent a copy to her parents back in Paducah or Peoria. Who did she say was standing beside her child? What did he represent? Was he one of "the natives?"

Our father's day usually began very early, before sunrise. That always seemed remarkable to me, though now, I realize that the sun rises rather late in the Islands, in comparison to the range possible in the northern latitudes. But he'd generally be gone by the time we were up and getting ready for school. Appropriately, it ended earlier, too, and he'd generally show up about three or four in the afternoon.

For a little boy, it was a very long day, and I didn't make it. Before the afternoon was over, I was sleeping in the front seat, next to my father. He had his hand on me. For a man not much given to expressions of affection, it was a large gesture.

Whenever our father came home from work, we children would watch for him to make the turn off Palolo Avenue, coming past the Apostolic Faith Church, then up along Pukele, across the park. The cry would be raised, "Father's coming!" and we raced out of the house to open the garage doors, pushing apart the two large doors hung on rollers. By then, he had come around on 7th Avenue, and he would back the truck into the cavernous garage.

There was one day when it was raining very hard, a torrential downpour. Our father thought he should drive us to school. Only until now did it occur to me that on such days, there was little point in his going out, since his customers would hardly want to go out in drenching rain just to buy a head of cabbage. So, there he was, at home, offering to take us to school. One reason I can remember this is that I was a little ashamed our father had such a mean profession, that his truck was so distinctive. It wasn't even nondescript; rather, it was altogether too articulate, with its canvas sides flapping in the wind.

Off we went to our schools, Barbara and me to St. Patrick's, Anita and Ronnie to the Sacred Hearts Academy, which was right across 6th Avenue, next to our school. All the students were scurrying into the school grounds, wearing their raincoats and carrying umbrellas, and not a few being driven up in cars. Here came the Changs, pulling up in their father's place of business. At least the older girls were able to ride in the cab and could make a proper exit through the passenger door; Barbara and I had to scramble out the back.

It isn't very pleasant to have to acknowledge such unworthy thoughts about one's father, but I don't suppose I am the first son ever to have these twinges of shame.

138

There was only one other instance of this discreditable emotion, but the instances were repeated with regularity. Every time I brought a report card home, I had to have my father sign it, and so, four times a year, I would have to return my card, and filling up the blanks in the back were my father's tortured scrawls, Chang Kwai. It was very clearly the hand of an illiterate man. All that, in an age when in fact the quality of one's penmanship served as an index to one's intellectual attainment.

I was so good at penmanship, at the repetitive drills—the vertical strokes, the loops that just touched the top and bottom of the lines—that I was deemed a superior student and ready for immediate advancement from 1st grade to 2nd grade. So I skipped a grade, and for the rest of my academic life, I was always the youngest in my class. In any event, it was your signature which betrayed who you were, and at that, my hand was never as good as that of my brothers', Anita's and Ronnie's. As usual, Barbara and I were more haphazard, less diligent, and were not true Palmer methodists.

Being ashamed of one's father is an unworthy thing, but life is fair. Years later, when I had my own brood of children, I can remember their expressing their deep misgivings about having to check into the Holiday Inn in Montreal carrying grocery bags, for we didn't have proper luggage. So I suggested a diversionary plan. We could check in and take the elevators in the lobby, but later, we could retrieve such belongings as we needed by going directly to the basement, where the van was parked. And at that, the van itself was almost as bad as our father's truck. It was just so big, it called attention to itself, and in the suburb where we lived, everyone knew the Chang van with its complement of children. They could be ashamed because we were always so conspicuous, at the very least.

What had closed my father's life as a wage earner was the phenomenon of the post-war world, the supermarket. And perhaps, it was also the end of the war, which inevitably took so many of his customers back to the mainland. It's very odd, but while I was older in 1945

139

than I was in 1941, I have very few memories of V.E. Day, when Germany surrendered. All I can recall is that the newspaper boys were asked to be excused from school early. The *Star-Bulletin* had an extra edition, and they needed the boys out on the streets hawking peace.

Our father could compete against the mom and pop grocery stores, aided by the large population of military dependents, but he was swept aside, along with the corner stores, by the appearance of the giant markets. It was a difficult thing for him, as it is for any person proud of his ability to meet financial responsibilities. A man's world was simpler then; all he had to do was to house and feed his family, and if possible, to provide for the education of his children. Chang Kwai did all that; he accomplished all that, but he was still relatively young, in his mid-fifties, and not an old man. But illness was added to the changing shape of retailing, and he was forced to give up his truck. He could not make enough to cover his gasoline expenses.

In one of those three years between my returning home and my leaving again, for graduate school, there was a summer when there was a miraculous event. The tree in the back yard, the *loongan see*, suddenly bore fruit. It was the first time in my whole life that it ever bore fruit. I had had the dried fruit before, where the flesh had shrivelled to a dark and chewy mass under the tough outer shell, enclosing the nut-like seed. It was alright, but like the dried lichee fruit, not really very interesting. The fresh fruit was another matter.

Smaller than the more famous delicacy, the lichee, loongan could nonetheless hold its own. The fruit was about as large as a bing cherry, covered by a semi-hard shell, which had to be peeled away. Like the lichee, the flesh of the fruit was a translucent white, dripping with a sweet nectar. After being introduced to the fresh fruit, I began to understand the tree's name, for the stone covered by the flesh was a glistening dark brown. Dragon's eyes, truly.

The tree spread about twenty feet in diameter, and it

was about that tall. Some of the branches hung over the
lath-covered greenhouse, others over the clothes lines. All
were laden with bunches of fruit in clusters, almost the
way grapes are. My mother and I spent a good part of the
morning picking the fruit, I up on a ladder or clambering
on the framework of the greenhouse, she on such boxes
and chairs that she could find a steady footing for. It
seems that we must have picked enough to fill several
large grocery bags. She was so excited that she insisted we
weigh the fruit. The truck was long gone, but we still had
the scale hanging in the garage. As I have no memory of
my father in any of this activity, I have to presume that he
was either in the Tripler Army General Hospital or inside,
in bed.

I cannot remember our mother ever showing so much
happiness and joy. For so much of her life, she wore the
face of responsibility and concern, encouragement or
disapproval. She was always working, being a mother,
homemaker and wife. It was the first time that she seemed
child-like. She was positive that the tree's sudden and
bountiful fecundity was an omen of good things to come.

Chapter Five

The period was 1956 to 1959, the years between my
return from St. Mary's College and my leaving for the
University of Wisconsin after the death of our father. At
that time, I was the only child living at home. Barbara was
teaching grammar school in New York City, Ronnie and
Toshio were in Madison, Anita, may have been in the
Philippines, though I think they by then had a house in
Kaneohe, and I believe all the brothers were in Honolulu. I
was just beginning my adult life, and our father was
ending his.

Living at home and teaching at my old high school, I
indulged my fancy and bought a used M.G., one of the
classic models, a TD, a car which still had fenders, which
had a hood like old cars did, that lifted up from the sides
of the engine block, like the wings of a bird, rather than

from the front, like Leviathan opening its jaws. It had vestigial running boards and an actual gas tank, mounted vertically on the back, upon which the exposed spare tire was attached. It was a car I took great pride in. For precisely that reason, one of my students in the high school vandalized it, puncturing the leather seats with a pocket knife. It was too bad, covering the leather with Naugahyde, but in the long run it didn't matter. I still enjoyed the car, even going so far as to install a Jensen supercharger.

My father was dying slowly, yet it was a good time for me. I had some money in my pocket. With a fellow teacher, I would go night clubbing on Waikiki Beach, making the various spots, from the Halekulani on the Ewa end of the strip to Queen's Surf, at the foot of Diamond Head. I bought a Nikon range finder camera, the model S2, then the SP, the last cameras of those designs before the introduction of the model F, the first Nikon reflex camera. I managed to put together a darkroom, complete with a Leitz enlarger.

In those salad days, it was my duty to administer the insulin injections for my father. Henry, being a dentist, had an autoclave. Every week, he would bring a fresh supply of syringes and needles, every one sterile. I would insert the needle through the rubber membrane to draw forth the requisite cubic centimeters of insulin, and then I would introduce it to our father's deltoid muscle, already scrubbed with alcohol. The day's syringe and needle were set aside, until the week's supply was used up, and Henry would pick them up and leave a fresh batch.

It must have been a very trying time for my father. I had always seen him as a strong man, although I doubt that he was much bigger than I am now. That's the way it is with children, isn't it, to enlarge reality, both the admirable and the fearful? But the man I ministered to seemed diminished in comparison to the man for whom we opened those garage doors. He would have to rely on me for support as he got on the bathroom scales. For as his debilitation advanced, I was asked to keep track of his weight and to record the volume of the fluids he eliminated. It surely must have been humiliating for him to urinate into a coffee can, knowing that his youngest child would then measure the volume, before flushing it all down the toilet. But it was necessary, to keep track of the edema.

Some time between the period when he lived in the garage and was so utterly dependent on me, having given up sucrose, sodium chloride and nicotine, his spirit may have broken.

There was one joy left to him, in those last three years. Henry and Amy would drop off their child, Estelle, Mee Yuk, to be cared for by our mother. Mee Yuk must have been two or three, a toddler. Her face was round, and her straight hair was gathered in two pigtails, separated by a part which ran from her brow to the nape. He loved that child dearly, not because she was herself more lovable than any of the other grandchildren, but because he himself was beginning to confront his mortality. He could then find joy in her burgeoning life.

In the afternoons, when I had completed my day's teaching, I would take our father and sometimes Mee Yuk for drives. In deference to his age, I would put the white top up, so that it would not be so windy. We would then drive up to Mount Tantalus, overlooking the city, where it is always cool, if somewhat damp. We would sit up there and look down on the Manoa Valley, where the University of Hawaii is located, then on down to the central district of the city, where King Street and Beretania formed the principal arteries, connecting the Diamond Head region with the farther reaches of Pearl Harbor.

On the way down, we could stop at one of several overlooks and see the small, extinct crater of the Punchbowl, now a national cemetery, the final home of so many fallen soldiers and sailors. We could enter the crater, passing the plumeria trees, which were commonly referred to as make man trees, because the Hawaiians favored those blossoms in their burial grounds. Hawaiian cemeteries always have plumeria trees.

Inside the Punchbowl, in the company of the dead, we could look down on the Ewa district, the Aloha Tower, where the great steamships once docked and disgorged their passengers. We could watch the planes take off from the Honolulu Airport; we could see Sand Island, Pearl Harbor, and Tripler Army General Hospital, the other pink structure in the city, the army's answer to the Royal Hawaiian Hotel on Waikiki Beach.

Our father and I had many drives together. Sometimes we would go to Diamond Head, to the overlook just past the lighthouse, above Doris Duke's estate on the water's edge. We could watch the surfers, never very many, compared to Waikiki Beach, but usually three or four, catching their waves for a ride to shore. As the force of the wave was dissipated, the surfer would move back on the board, kick its nose in the air, and swivel it around, toward the horizon, then paddle out again, belly on the board, back arched and head up toward the place where other surfers were sitting easy on their boards, waiting for a wave big enough to justify the effort of a surge of power, to match the speed of the incoming wave.

Sometimes I would take him to Ala Moana Park, the site of the annual picnic of the Oo Sack village. As I understand it, everyone from the old village was inevitably and irrevocably bound to each other, and these binding ties were reaffirmed by the picnic. It was a pot-luck affair with the standard Fourth of July games, volleyball, sack races, three-legged races, and the like. Was it fun? Yes and no. It was just something you did. You didn't question or argue. You just went and had what fun you could.

When I brought my father back to the Ala Moana Park, he would sit on the sand and look out on the calm lagoon, formed by an artificial reef. The waves broke beyond the barrier; within the enclosed waters, it was as calm as though it were an indoor pool. Sitting on the warm sand, the sun beginning to set over Haleiwa, shaded by his straw hat, he would let sand run between his fingers, puff on his pipe, and say nothing. His silence was not strange. He never said much.

I would drive our father out past Diamond Head, along the Kalanianaole Highway, past the Kuapa Pond, up Koko Head, to Hanauma Bay, where we would sit, looking down on the quiet enclosure of water. Now, Hanauma Bay is a preserve, no fishing is permitted, whether by hook and line or spear. Full of coral reefs, it is a favorite of tourists who come with their snorkeling gear and bags of food for the fish. The fish seem to know that no one will harm them; they approach the swimmers, poor impostors of the aquatic species with their masks over their faces, flippers on their feet, and breathing tubes in their mouths. The fish come, knowing that the curious creature has a bag of old bread or frozen peas or corn. These, released in the water, trigger a feeding frenzy, and the snorkeler is surrounded by fish who act as though they had not eaten in months, but which probably did exactly the same thing two minutes before. It is the Hawaiian version of the pigeons on the square at St. Mark's in Venice, where tourists buy bags of grain to scatter, or even better, for sprinkling on their hair and shoulder, attracting a flock of birds. Always, a photographer is there to get the picture.

We would drive on, past the bay, the site of so many grammar school picnics, to the Halona Blowhole, Oahu's modest answer to Old Faithful. If the waves were right, they would crash upon the volcanic shore with a fury that would be captured in some unseen fissures to erupt with violence, perhaps fifty feet into the air. And if the Blowhole was quiet, perhaps you could see the island of Molokai, almost thirty miles away, Molokai, where Father Damien cared for the lepers, where Anita's husband grew up, where annually, there is a race of Hawaiian canoes, rendered stable for crossing the ocean by their outriggers.

Sometimes we would go a few miles farther, toward Waimanalo and Bellows Air Force Base, stopping at Sandy Beach. Sandy Beach, during the war, always carried signs warning the swimmers of the treacherous waters. The military was protecting their mainland soldiers. We would leave the highway, and we would clamber among the volcanic rocks, eroded by the sea and forming little tidal pools where small fish and crabs would be trapped. The landscape was always interesting, for the lava rocks were dark and black, rough in outline and painful to the bare foot. The trapped waters were clear, and one could see the little fishes and crabs. Beyond, there was the Pacific, pounding with its unrelenting and gentle energy. At Sandy Beach, the body surfers rode the waves near the shore.

In all the hours I spent with our father, we never spoke. I don't feel guilty about that; after all, one just did not speak with one's father. Besides, I would not have known what to say, what to ask. Now, past fifty, I can fault myself for not having pressed a conversation, however limited by my ignorance of Chinese, but I wasn't past fifty then. I was only in my early twenties. I was doing what I could to make him comfortable, to help him pass the hours. It did not occur to me that I would one day want to know what he was thinking. That's really why I never asked.

In all that time, I came to see our father in a new and unexpected way. He was weak; he relied on my arm to get in and our of my car; I had to watch him as he moved among the rocks, occasionally lending support. This was not the man I remembered from my childhood, energetic and resourceful, in command of whatever situation he was in. Chinese daddies could do everything except to live forever.

Chinese Hot Pot

Wing Tek Lum

My dream of America
is like dá bìn lòuh
with people of all persuasions and tastes
sitting down around a common pot
chopsticks and basket scoops here and there
some cooking squid and others beef
some tofu or watercress
all in one broth
like a stew that really isn't
as each one chooses what he wishes to eat
only that the pot and fire are shared
along with the good company
and the sweet soup
spooned out at the end of the meal.

The Poet Imagines
His Grandfather's Thoughts
on the Day He Died   Wing Tek Lum

This is the first year
the Dragon Eyes tree has ever borne fruit:
let us see what this omen brings.
Atop one of its exposed roots
a small frog squats, not moving, not even blinking.
I remember when my children were young
and this whole front yard was a taro patch:
we would take them out at night with a lantern
blinding the frogs just long enough
to sneak a hook up under the belly.
In those days we grew taro
as far as the eye could see;
I even invented a new kind of trough
lined inside with a wire mesh
so we could peel the skins with ease.
The King bought our poi,
and gave me a pounder one day.
It is made of stone,
and looks like the clapper of a bell, smooth and heavy.
I keep it in my bedroom now—there—on the dresser.
The fish we call Big Eyes
lies on an oval plate beside it.
I have not been hungry today.
The full bowl of rice attracts a fly
buzzing in anticipation.
I hear the laughter of one of my grandchildren
from the next room: which one is it?
Maybe someday one of them will think of me
and see the rainbows that I have seen,
the opium den in Annam that frightened me so,
my mother's tears when I left home.

Dear ancestors, all this is still one in my mind.

Taking Her to
the Open Market

Wing Tek Lum

Scales glisten;
pink whiskers jut out.
Some are the color
of mud, others
recall the embroidery
of coats placed
on babes one month old.
Fat, round, small:
they lay on the crushed
ice, stall after stall.

"Look at the fresh fish!"
I exclaim, eager to impress
on her our respect
for the old
ways, and that I know
how to tell the firmness
a poached flesh will have
by the bulging
of its eyes, the blood
in the gills.

"They are dead,"
she replies. Taken aback,
I see
through her Hong Kong eyes
that fresh
means leaning over
a galvanized pan, eyeing
closely through the running
water at that
cluster of darting
shadows, seeking out the one
swimming most
vigorously: in demonstration

that it
has not yet
passed the point of no return.

"We have,"
I mutter, "killed off
more than germs."

Juk

Wing Tek Lum

was what I used to eat
a lot of—like everyday
I'd cross the street to Hong Wah's
for a take-out. On seeing me
the owner by the register
would try to outguess me.
Waaht Gāi Jūk, she'd bellow
in a knowing way,
as if it were my name.

It was a game we played.
Depending on my whim
I'd simply nod my head, assenting,
or correct her, smiling:
Fó Ngáap—to which she'd call
the order out again,
so that the waiter down the aisle
could write it for the kitchen.

Later, if she got a chance,
she'd go back personally.
You could see her through the open door:
first, with a ladle scooping
the soup, a light sprinkle
of scallions, and then the quick plop
of a handful of duck, chopped
in chunks, covered
I knew with lots of skin.

She would fill out a few orders
like this: soup
in the red containers, the dishes
of rice and of noodles
into white boxes. In turn,
they would all be dropped
into bags, which she'd carry

—maybe three to an arm—
as she rushed, waddling,
up to the front.
                    Sometimes,
I wondered if the hectic pace
would kill her in a year.
At other times I felt:
she's probably now a millionaire.
No one has made as good
a juk since then. I hope it tasted
as good to her
                    as it did to me.

T-Bone Steak   Wing Tek Lum

The Chinese cut their meat before
sautéing with
vegetables cut up
the same
way, deeming those individual
portions of steak,
served American-
style, extravagant, dull,
unsociable,
and requiring too
much effort with the knife
while eating.

My father on occasion
brought home
one T-bone. *Máang fó, nyùhn
yàuh*, he cautioned:
heat
the skillet first,
the oil you pour just
before you lay
the steak on.
Delegated, I eased the full
slab on with wooden
chopsticks (forks and
other metal
objects puncture). The black
cast iron
splattered oil. My mother
usually told me to
put on
my shirt.
I lowered the
flame, and
every so often nudged
at the recessed

areas near the bone against
the pan's flat
surface. We
liked our
meat medium-rare, five
minutes to a
side at
most. At the chopping
block, I sliced off long
chunks, a half inch
thick, quickly
serving them on a platter ready
to eat, among
our other
sung, before the blood
oozed out completely.

No, it was not
Chinese, much less
American, that pink piece
sitting in my rice
bowl. It was,
simply, how our family
ate, and I
for one am grateful for
the difference.

Kindergarten

Wing Tek Lum

After one month we've got the rituals down pat.
Entering the school
we drive over the first bump in the road
and I announce that it's time to get ready
though she really doesn't need to be reminded.
I angle over to the left lane
where the kindergarten gets dropped off
and she disengages the buckle of her seat belt.
She's already been riding in the back seat
so she can get out on the left side by herself.
And then we hit the second bump
and I turn my face slightly towards her
and she leans forward from the back
with the car in mid-bump
to kiss me a goodbye on my cheek.
It is small and soft, and slightly cold and wet.
And then we drive up to the end of the car line
and wait for our turn nearing the gate.
She always tells me to move up closer
to where the gate is
but at some point I say that she should get out.
She opens the door by herself and gets down
shouldering her little book bag
stuffed with the day's assortment of papers and toys.
As she pushes the car door shut
I warn her about her footing
worried that she might slip off the curb.
We watch each other for a while
she walking along the sidewalk
and me keeping pace with her in the car.
We give each other knowing looks
and she turns to enter the playground
where all the kids are.
My job is now done I know
and I ease back into the drive through lane.
Still as I do I cannot help

but try to catch one last glimpse of her
in my side view mirror.
She is walking over to her friends
with her back towards me.
Somehow I can sense
that she has forgotten about me already.
The morning is fresh and clear
and I drive away with only a father's regret.

Poetic License

Wing Tek Lum

Once I wrote about my daughter
and how I took her to school everyday.
She would kiss me on my cheek
in the car just before she got dropped off.
And I showed this poem to my friends
one night when they came over.
And being friends I guess behind my back
they checked out my version against hers.
My daughter is so young and innocent
—and though of course I am all for her
growing up with a mind of her own
she does not yet know
how a family needs to stick together.
She denied outright that part I wrote
about how her kisses were so moist.
It was instead my cheeks
she claimed that were wet
from the fact that I shower in the mornings.
How embarrassing to be undercut
by my own daughter—even when she is wrong.
I am the poet who is supposed
to tell the truth about life and art.
Who are you going to believe otherwise?

Apparition Beryl Blaich

The rains   that hid the comet   brought gardenias.
  Bushes   which had been spindly sparse and yellow leafed
    Fulled   on the schedule they steer   flowers
      Pulling their course from nowhere
        We could visit.

First   new leaves   so dark green and shining
  They are black impenetrable and infinite   new leaves
    Dark and shining so   they make light   as they bunch
      Cluster and swell the tight   whorled comas
        Which some energy pushes toward the sun.

One morning   the flowers arrive their perihelion.
  A slit of white peeking visible yawns   unfurls
    Wider   now blazes   whiteness
      Streaming fragrance.

I pick the gardenias. Daily relieve the bushes
  Of their astronomical burden I harvest deluge basketfuls.
    The house is soaked with sultry gardenia incense rising
      From china bowls from tea cups   and jelly jars
        Off the dining table   next to beds
          By the sinks   on toilets.

    This outfragrancing   tips   inclines
  rushes me in ellipses of recollection. I am in
my parents' backyard in Manoa, picking gardenias off the bush
  that is as old as this old white house.
    The bush is the center of this valley,
  equidistant from each blue-green mountainwall,
and I am the flower in this bowl my mother places in the fancy
  downstairs bathroom she calls the powder room
    and has papered in cream and gold.
    The gardenias die, turning gold and cream,
losing their moisture but not their sweet rich smell
  so we are wealthy as my pake friend Patty

who has a gardenia hedge, a Lincoln
Continental and a plate of manapua and pepeiau
from Mauna Kea Street where the flower vendor lei sellers keep
  galvanized buckets filled with water and gardenia buds
    rolled like sushi in wide green ti leaves.
The flowers wait for evening to burst into star
ornaments in the hair of the night ladies of the Hotel Street bars,
  of Harlem jazz joints, of Paris nightclubs
    where Billie Holliday wears a single blossom
and long white gloves. She is singing like a saxophone
lavish buzzy, ritzy boozy and I am orbiting reeling dizzy drunk
  on this gardenia nectar astral travel

And unless I live to be one hundred and fourteen
  I will never see that comet. But the gardenias and me,
    Our paths intersect in April.

Social Graces   Sue Lin Chong

When I was six years old my father decided to
relocate our family—me, my brother who is three years
younger, and our mother, from Hawaii to the suburbs of
New Jersey. I had never heard the term then, but
Moorestown is one of the conservative "bedroom
communities" of Philadelphia, which lay 20 minutes
across the river. During those first months our father
explained this move offered more challenging
opportunities for his medical practice and we'd have fun
playing in the crunching, dusty leaves in the autumn and
in the snow in winter. All this turned out to be true, but
along the way it also meant not seeing my cousins and
grandparents, adjusting to a small Quaker community
where we couldn't see movies or shop on Sundays, and
where the adults couldn't buy liquor on any day. It also
meant being the only Chinese family in the entire town.

In the late 1950's, Moorestown had the look of a
near-Norman Rockwell painting—not as crisp and glowing
as the real thing, but close enough, with its central Main
Street, stately pin oak and sugar maple trees shading the
cars leisurely traveling between the neat homes centered
on square grassy lots, and a small congregation of
shopkeepers in the middle of town. During these years
before the town became ringed with shopping malls, the
only place in town to shop for clothes was Weinberg's
Store. Weinberg's Store was actually two tiny stores,
separated by an alley—women's and girls' clothes on the
left, men's and boys' clothes on the right.

The stores fascinated me and my brother. They were
run by Sophie Weinberg and her younger brother
Ben—the first Jews we had ever known. At our age we
didn't quite know what Jews did or believed in, other than
we were hustled out of the store late Friday afternoons
because it closed a bit earlier that day and that when we
cruised by the store on our bikes Saturday morning, the
Weinbergs were never there. Other than the weekends, it

seemed to us the Weinbergs ran their entire lives around their stores.

And what stores they were! In the fifteen years our mother took us there, there was only the most imperceptible changes in the merchandise—mainly in the colors of the sturdy, no-nonsense clothes that appeared on the faded mannequins in the cramped display windows. Weinberg's specialized in the basic clothes every mother dressed her growing children in—nothing too fancy and nothing too expensive or frivolous. The most fascinating part of Weinberg's was that each store was in total chaos.

Heaps of plastic BVD packages precariously balanced on metal racks, threatening to crash down on customers' heads and mismatched socks tangled with white cotton T-shirts in plastic bins on the boys' side of the store run by Ben Weinberg. On the girls' side, run by Sophie, Jantzen training bras with their stretchy cups outlined with thin straps were strewn among pastel nylon panties.

What made the Weinbergs so mysterious was that they always knew exactly where everything was. Also, the middle-aged brother and sister were never seen in the other's store and my brother and I concluded that this must be part of being Jewish—that men and women must be strictly separated and not interfere in each other's lives. During those years when we constantly schemed of ways to torment each other, we agreed that maybe being Jewish wouldn't be too bad, if it meant not having to live peaceably with one another. We later learned the Weinbergs had only each other in this world and lived in a small apartment at the edge of town. My brother and I eyes one another uneasily—did this mean we would grow old and musty-smelling together and faithfully carry out mysterious religious ceremonies every Friday night?

During the years I grew up in Moorestown, the reminders I had of being Chinese slowly fell away each season we stayed away from Honolulu. There was only one event that occurred every Sunday morning that jarred me back into remembering we were a Chinese family. This was our weekly trip into Philadelphia's Chinatown to buy fresh vegetables, oyster sauce, dim sum, and roasted pork. The visits into the Chinese groceries were a treat and the smells of the glistening, crispy duck skin and sounds of meat being sliced neatly away by a cleaver brought back the thoughts of my grandparents and their trips to Oahu Market. But beyond these memories of Hawaii, the shopping expeditions invariably ended up in a battle between my mother and me over my having to eat bitter melon.

I didn't care which way my mother devised to cook the bitter melon—it was foul-tasting and the ugliest vegetable I had ever seen in my life. "I hate this stuff!" I told my parents. "It's shaped like those rats I've seen in my biology books, and it's bumpy, it's green, and it tastes terrible—please don't make me eat it."

"It's good for you," my mother always replied. "That bitter taste is quinine, it's good for headaches."

"But I don't have a headache," I moaned. "I never get headaches!"

Meanwhile, my brother who would rather take in my desperate protests in silence and eventually eat the bitter melon begrudgingly, just stared at me across the table, hoping for once I could invent a better argument that would save us from eating another portion. My efforts never worked. We were condemned to eat bitter melon once a week. What was worse was that we knew we were the only children in town who had to do this. And this was the most humiliating part of being the only Chinese for miles around.

A few years after many confrontations with the bitter melon, my brother and I experienced a different ordeal we found even more humiliating. Our school was about a mile from our home and we usually walked our separate ways after school with our own friends. This one day, we happened to meet at one of the shortcuts the kids in our neighborhood created through a shaded orchard right-of-way and fell into step.

Along the way, we passed a group of junior high boys, lounging under the trees. "Hey chinks!" one of them taunted.

"Yeah, chinks," another one joined, and before we knew it, this group sprung up and began to approach us. Without a word, the tallest boy began to vigorously tug the corners of his eyes up and down, and the rest of his group followed his silent actions.

My brother and I gaped in astonishment at this grotesque pantomime. Before we could turn and run, we were surrounded by several of these pale, tall boys, each manipulating their eyes into slits, bobbing their heads toward us in unison.

Before the group closed off its silent circle, I swung my arms and brought my plaid bookbag down squarely on the nearest boy's head. Thwack! The pantomime stopped and then I saw my brother take off, breaking through the stunned circle toward the end of the path. I followed as fast as I could, not daring to turn around to see if they were behind us. Most of the boys in the broken circle were strangers to me, but as I raced home, I caught a glimpse out of the corner of my eye of our paperboy among the group.

We never really talked about what happened once we got home, but were relieved that the other one was there. That incident had caught us off guard. Until that time, we never considered ourselves as outsiders to our schoolmates. As we later dwelled on this separately, the fact sunk in that we weren't round-eyed and pale white like our classmates. This realization was different from the bitter taste of the melon we still had to eat, but nonetheless, it stung and stuck to our insides.

A few weeks after our confrontation, we noticed something new in the Sophie Weinberg side of Weinberg's Store. Miss Weinberg hired a salesclerk named Maria Petrodopolous. Maria, her mother, and her sister were recent immigrants from Greece and soon replaced the Weinbergs as the new curiosity for my brother and me. Maria followed Miss Weinberg around the disarray of her store, eager to meet the good customers, greeting them extravagantly in an overly loud voice. In contrast to the sad-eyed, dark Miss Weinberg, Maria was overly made-up, with heavy pancake foundation applied to her homely face which was marked by a sharp hooked nose, and furry facial hair that the foundation tried to conceal. What was most astonishing to me was her clothing—as my mother said, Maria "poured" herself into a tight black skirt that cupped her behind like a question mark, topped by a clingy banlon short-sleeved sweater that outlined the concentric stitching on her bra. Despite her garish appearance, I often overheard her speaking in a breathless voice to her sister that she knew several of the passing men who bought their newspapers next door at Olliver's Sundries had been eyeing her and she would quickly glance from the receiver to the display window to see if anyone was staring back at her. However, I never saw any of her stares returned by the passersby nor did I sense Maria had any friends her age in her new surroundings. During one trip into Sophie Weinberg's store after school, I noticed Maria standing in the small alley next to the stores, chatting with the boy who delivered our evening newspapers. My brother and I later learned through our sleuthing that Maria and the paperboy occasionally met in the alley during her afternoon break and we sometimes heard her extravagant laugh float through the open skylight of the Weinberg's store. But a few weeks later, we overheard Miss Weinberg lecture Maria that too much time was being spent on the afternoon breaks and from then on, we never saw Maria and the paperboy together again.

Just when Maria and her odd-looking family ceased to be a curiosity to us, an astonishing event occurred. One evening as my brother and I were doing our homework before dinner, the phone rang. I answered it. It was Maria, in breathless and loud tones, who asked to speak to my mother. Puzzled, I handed her the receiver.

After a silence, I heard my mother say, "No, I'm sorry. There must be a mistake. I'm so sorry. No, no."

Sensing something strange was happening, I motioned for my brother to get into the kitchen and we watched as my mother slowly hung up the receiver, a perplexed but controlled look on her face.

"How odd," she said, turning back to prepare our dinner. "That was Maria asking what time she should be here tonight—what ever gave her the idea she was invited to dinner with us?" My brother and I turned to each other in amazement—not that it would be such a bad idea, perhaps, but how did this misunderstanding come about? And what had my mother said to her?

"Of course I told her she couldn't come over here. There must have been a terrible mistake."

One week later, my mother learned that Maria was the victim of a joke played by our paperboy, the same silent junior high kid who had confronted my brother and me in the right-of-way. After Maria was warned not to linger over her afternoon breaks with him, he had run into her along Main Street and turned as he passed her on his bicycle, "Hey Maria, Mrs. Chong has invited you to dinner next Friday!" And then he sped away. And Maria believed him and called us, only to be told there must be a misunderstanding.

From that day on, things were different when we visited Weinberg's Store. Everytime my mother and I went to the girls' side, Maria would duck into the back room and come out only if Miss Weinberg became confused over where the newest shipments had been stored. Maria never met my mother's eyes and it was only then I saw that behind her loud voice and swooping gestures, was the look of someone who didn't fit in and was pinched by loneliness and her strange surroundings.

I have often wondered what would have happened if my mother recovered quickly on the phone when Maria called us and we all shared a meal that night. No, I eventually realized, that couldn't be. Because even though our family and her family were the different ones in our town, as long as we were planted firmly on the opposite sides of the Weinberg's Store's messy counters, there were social graces to observe and a line to be drawn.

Sleeper

Sheryl Dare

Your dark head
sinking slowly, swaying
into night's moist gravity:
watching you, I wish
I were the goddess
whose buddhist mercy alone
could turn all bad dreams
into good, threading
ropes of light
around your soft meanderings,
your still, patterned flowerings
of sleep;

for I know,
when the camphor-
breaths begin to lift
evenly off your back,
when your eyes shift upwards
into their sockets
to squint through the thin,
narrow bone-light of dreams,
I know that you are searching again
for the one most like yourself—

the Onward One, the one
that is waiting to take
you out to sea, the Hidden
One calling you over the old
stones, the dry places and
scooped-out cliffs you've forgotten
you've walked on before—

so fierce the way
your quiet face lurches
forward in the darkness
coming to meet itself!

I pull the blanket over you,
reach out to feel
the animal sweetness
of your hand
and dream and dream I am
standing with you
on the wave's edge, watching
how you bring yourself to birth
each night.

For Tom (1945-1975)　　　　Sheryl Dare

Afterward, long
after we have taken
the bits of spine
and skin and burnt
hair and woven them
together and thrown
them into the sea, I will
pick a shell from the foam.
And I will hold it
to the light to see
its thin white armature
coiled around the dry piece
of flesh once known as the
animal. Animal: because
it once quivered, and resisted,
and submitted to the probing
of hands.
And I will hold it against
my lips, because it is
cool, and has the same shape
of breath when released
into sound;
and then to my ears, because
the sound will be the faraway
humming of your own
tiny bones in my hand.

No Mistaking   Darrell H.Y. Lum

"Dis morning, ho, erryting buckaloose. I thought I
was gone wit da wind. Dey come massage me. Ho da
rough dey rub me. I donno how come dey so rough. And
all kine doctors stand around my bed. Four doctors one
time. My doctor ask me, 'Mr. Lee, you know who I am?'

"I tell, 'Of course. You my doctor. And dat my sister
Florence and my brother-in-law Ed and my brother
Howard and Irene.' Get four doctors checking up on me
and da man nurse rubbing me and massaging me rough. I
donno why dey so rough. They push me all over.

"Chee, dey went call everybody to da hospital like
dat, just like when my mother died. Chee...maybe I was
little mo gone wit da wind, yeah? Otherwise dey no call
up everybody like dat, yeah?

"Chee, maybe little mo gone wit da wind," he circled
his hand in the air I imagined the wind.

"But now I feel okay. But dis morning, gone with da
wind. Huh, da Buddha, Kwan Yin, look aftah me. No come
fo me yet.

"Thirty five years I live by myself. Take care myself..."
he trailed off and looked out the window. The view
outside the hospital room was of exhaust pipes from the
kitchen and the boiler room and across the way,
windowless concrete walls. "But me," he continued, "I have
self control...no have temptation."

"Plenty ladies like marry me you know. Dey pinch
my ear, pinch my cheek, pinch down there," he pointed
toward his groin and grinned.

"But I no damn fool. If I marry now, I gotta give half
da house to her. What fo, when I got em so dat da two
girls, my two granddaughters, get da house when I die. I
no need wife. Night time, I get lonely, I hug my blanket,
hug my pillow, dat's all.

"Me I like girls you know. Boys, you tell dem
someting dey say 'yeah, yeah' but in their mind dey fight

you.

"Well I'm eighty-eight years old. At least I got to see my granddaughter get married. Japanee boy. Well, dat's okay you know. I took care of dem when dey were babies you know. Later on they can have dis house. Good girls. Good to have girls.

"I think dis American food they give me better fo me, you know. One scoop rice only, little bit meat, vegetables. Me, I like eat *hahm gnee*, salt fish you know. Ho dat buggah make you eat rice...

"Now no mo *hahm gnee*, no mo *hau see*, oysters, yeah. Heh, I used to steam da *hau see* and eat with rice. Put *hau yau* on top. Ho, da good dat. No good eat dat kine, too salty, bad for da high blood pressure but I like eat dat, boy. Da social worker like me go inside one of dose homes, but I no can eat dat kine Filipino food. You know da Filipinos run da nursing homes nowdays...ho, I no can eat dat kine. I tell her, 'Yeah, yeah,' but I thinking, 'I not going to dat kine place, eat Filipino food.' They no can make me go dat kine place, yeah?

"Waste time sit around here. I told my doctor, 'What fo I stay in here only sit around. I can sit around at home. Same ting!' I went call up my sister Florence dis morning, tell her to bring my clothes and my wallet. Mo bettah I catch da cab go home! She told me I no can go until da doctor say I can go home. 'He said pretty soon,' I told her. Pretty soon."

*****

At home, Uncle Kam Chong looked even thinner than when he was in the hospital. Pale and thin, just flesh hanging on a skeleton after almost being "gone with the wind." He had always been skinny. But now he was so thin, I couldn't imagine him anymore with one of those white paper caps serving up sodas and malts behind the fountain at Benson-Smith Drugstore downtown. It was one of those fountains with the tall swivel stools and the

170

chrome gooseneck spigots: water, soda water, and Coke. I remembered barely being able to see over the counter waiting for my Coke float with an extra cherry and watching Uncle's ears. He had interesting ears, just right it seemed for holding up the paper cap, and long floppy lobes which years later explained the funny kinship I had always felt between my uncle and the Kwan Yin statue at the Academy of Arts. There always was a peaceful comfortableness about being around both of them.

And now, long after Benson-Smith and bussing dishes at a whole string of Chinese restaurants, those same ears held up a felt hat with a fancy feather hatband. In the summer, it was the cooler woven straw one. You could track his comings and goings in Chinatown by that hat. He was so short and stooped that you could only find him by his hat: walking the streets, stopping to look in store windows, to peer down alleys. Or by the cloud of pipe smoke in Wing Wah Jade where he sat with the owner and thumbed the bas relief carving on the new jade pieces.

"I used to catch da bus erryday to Chinatown. Walk around. Me I no like stay home. Catch da bus, walk around. Chew da fat little while at da jewelry store. Den come home. Sundays, I catch bus go church. I gotta go around. No can stay home. No can now. Maybe I gotta stay home little while. Chee, I miss dat. Pretty soon maybe I can go again. Now no can.

"Now I'm all right. Maybe later I gotta go Palolo Old Man Home. But now I'm okay. Maybe one, two years from now. I donno. Ho boy, nine hundred bucks a month you know. Dem *pakes* wanna cheat you, you see. They get anykine donations from errybody but dey still wanna charge you nine hundred bucks a month. Ho boy."

We sat there, not looking at each other. We both looked out the window. The window screen needs cleaning, I thought. I scanned the coffee table pushed up against the corner of the living room. It was full of old photographs: his sons, his granddaughters. I found a picture of me and my brother. I must've been four or five, the "baby" of the family and had my hair slicked down and was sucking my left thumb. He complained about the weather and his arthritis.

"I'm eighty-eight years old last week. Eighty-nine, Chinese calendar. All my life I never had dis kine trouble. Now erry morning I take five pills. Damn pills cost me seventy bucks, you know. And dis damn weather...my arthritis...all sore ovah here in my shoulder and in my hands."

He stretched his fingers out wide, then closed his hand. I noticed his thumb: big and knobby and calloused still from tamping hot pipe tobacco. He wore two pieces of jade pinned to his undershirt and when we talked he turned his good ear toward me. His earlobes bobbed and wobbled as he talked about his aches and he massaged the base of his thumb at the joint. The wind in the valley had picked up, he must've felt the rain coming. It was time to go.

*****

It was two months later after a couple of false starts and, I imagined, quite a bit of grumbling, Uncle Kam Chong made the move a couple of miles up the road to the "old man home."

Palolo Chinese Home. It was at the back of the valley where the road began to curve around and started back out again. The place was clean, plain, and functional. It was strikingly Chinese: layers of blood red paint on the columns, dark green trim and light green and white walls. There were two dormitories with upturned eaves, men's and women's, separated by a cafeteria.

It was quiet when I drove up. The men ringed the outside of their building just sitting or smoking in chairs pushed up against the walls. It was a quiet bunch. No loud talking like in Chinatown or shouting like at the mah jong games or arguing like at the fish market. Mostly everyone was just sitting outside, two or three chairs apart or inside the lounge watching TV. It looked like I was the only visitor that day. Uncle Kam Chong was sitting right outside the front door, cane in his lap, unlit pipe in his hand. He didn't recognize me until I got closer and I called out, "*Kau Goong*, Uncle. How you?"

"Heh, I'm okay. I'm okay, now."

"How's this place? How's the food?"

"Not bad. Food not bad. I eat everything. Fresh air."

"Lousy," the man two seats down muttered to himself loud enough for us to hear. I looked at him and he looked away and lit a cigarette. "Same ole ting for six years," he offered to no one in particular. Uncle Kam Chong ignored the interruption and continued, "I eat good, eat regular. Dey no need wash my dish, I eat um so clean!"

"So far so good, I never relax like dis before, no need worry about cook, about wash dishes. They serve you."

Another resident shuffled up and smiled at me. He pointed his cane and introduced the old timer who didn't like the food, Mr. Chun, to me. Then he introduced himself, Mr. Tam.

"Yeah," Mr. Tam said. "This is a good place. Anything you want, they get for you. The ladies very helpful." He beamed at us.

"Come watch boxing on TV," he said. He jabbed the air with his cane in the direction of the lounge.

It had started to drizzle. A light mist. Mr. Tam urged us to sit inside the lounge, "Much more comfortable and don't get wet."

Uncle pointed out that we were under the eaves.

"No, thank you," I said. "It's dry out here."

Mr. Chun muttered, "Dis only mosquito rain, rain little bit and then pau. At's all."

Mr. Tam tugged at his knitted hockey cap and pulled it down securely over his ears. Except for the cap, everyone was dressed nearly the same: bundled up in long trousers and an aloha shirt topped by a collarless, button-up sweater. Mr. Chun was one of the few who was sweaterless. Just a white tee-shirt and trousers.

"You should wear one of these hats," Mr. Tam

instructed Uncle. "Keep warm."

"Yeah, maybe later on I get one," Uncle said.

"No, no. Just ask the ladies. They bring fo you. Free."
Mr. Tam tugged again at his cap to make his point. "Free."

Mr. Tam beamed a toothless grin at me. Reassuringly
he said, "This place good. Everybody is nice. You come
back learn Chinese," he added as he shuffled off.

Uncle fingered his pipe. It was unlit and empty.

"Hey, you need anything. You got enough tobacco?"

"Yeah, I need tobacco. I had one big can but I donno
where I put um. And matches, I need matches. I used to
have someplace. I donno where I put um..."

"Next time I'll bring you some matches," I said.

"Yeah, one box nuff. Sometimes I forget nowdays.
Ho, the other day I forget where I put my teeth. Come
time to eat, I no can find um. Ho, I worry like hell. No mo
teeth, no can eat, you know. Later on, somebody find um
in da bathroom. Good ting. I no can remember where I
left um. Drop inside da toilet you know! Ho, da lady go
soak um in solution fo me. One whole day she soak um.
Otherwise, no can eat! Lucky."

"Lucky you found um," I repeated.

"Lady. Lady find um." It was Mr. Chun again. "Da
lady janitor found um. Me too, sometimes forget things,
nowdays."

Uncle said, "One of the cafeteria ladies told me she
hold my teeth for me. Whenever I need um, she bring um.
'Nah,' I told her. I no like bother."

"You gotta take care now. No lose um again. Maybe
better to let the lady hold um for you," I worried aloud.

"Hey, when you gonna take over the cafeteria?" I
teased. "J'like the old days at Benson-Smith. You used to
be manager or something, huh?"

"Manager, buyer, everything I was. Work there fo
forty years. Start off at two dollars a week."

"A week?"

"A week. After the fourth grade, after my father died,
I went work. Make some money. Help out the family. I no
need too much. Only go movies now and then. Cowboy

movies. Shucks.

"Pretty soon they let me run the lunch counter. Big place you know. Three hundred one time can sit down. They try anykine, you know. They bring in all kine guys but they no can make money. Only I could. One time they bring in three *haole* guys from the mainland to watch me fo one month because they no believe my profit so high: seventy, seventy-two, seventy-four percent. At the end of the month they ask me. 'Lee, how you do it?' I says, 'I donno.' You think I gonna tell them? Baloney! How come they ask me!"

"So how you did it, Uncle?" I asked.

"You know, only three things you gotta watch: the girls no put too much, you know, when they make samwich they put two or three slice meat. Next, watch so they no eat too much. You know, sometimes they make two, three samwich for themself and they take one, two bite then leave um alone. You see, how much waste, yeah? And den you watch they no charge their friends or they make something big and only charge little bit. Dat's all. Dat and at the end of the month, no good have too much inventory. You order heavy at the beginning and den cut down, cut down so by the end of the month you get almost nothing. Dat's all."

"You're all right, Uncle."

"Yeah, you watch the inventory. All my meat, one size. I regulate the machine to slice, you see. One pound ham supposed to get twelve slices. Huh. And they ask me, 'How you do it, Lee?' Dey no can get seventy percent profit. When you only get forty, fifty percent that no good you know, something wrong."

Uncle fingered his empty pipe.

"Let's go look for your tobacco," I said. "You can show me your room."

There were four beds in each room. Each corner identical with a clothes locker and small table next to each bed. Looking for the tobacco was like looking through a locker at an elementary school. Little treasures mixed in with the necessities, all conspicuously marked. My mother

175

must've done it when he moved in. I recognized her fat, round script on every handkerchief, shirt, pants and pair of underwear. There weren't too many places to look. I stopped myself from suggesting that we go look in the community bathroom down the hall. Maybe the tobacco can had ended up in the same place as his teeth. I found a brown paper sack full of boiled peanuts. Uncle Kam Chong offered them to me when I showed him the bag. I sniffed at it suspiciously.

"Where did you get these?" I asked.

"My friend gave me," he answered a little defensively. "One old guy. One Chinese guy. He say he know me. But I no can remember him. He know me. But I no recognize him. Ah..."

"When did he come?"

"Oh, couple days ago."

"Maybe you ought to give this to the kitchen. They can keep um in the icebox for you. So it doesn't spoil." I sniffed the package again.

"It's all right. No sour."

I poured a handful out. Uncle cracked one open and chewed. We settled down in the chairs right outside his room.

"So what, get activities. Things to do?"

"Yeah, they get exercise class. One lady, I donno how she know my name, she tell me, 'Eh Mr. Lee, let's go exercise.' I say, 'No thank you, I too old.' "

"But if you exercise you sleep good, you know," I suggested.

"Hah, next day you get up, you all ache all over," he laughed.

"So what, that lady your new girlfriend now?"

"Naw. I don't believe those kine now. Girlfriend. Only mouth, girlfriend. They try to skin you, boy. Danger, you know. Some of dem smooth-talker, you know." He paused to reflect and chewed on a few more peanuts.

"Well, depend on the man," he continued. "You bite, you trapped already. One time one lady tell me, 'Eh, Lee, you funny kine of man. You funny kine of man.' "

"Why she call you funny kine?"

"I donno. Maybe because I no like marry her. Shucks. You tink I damn fool?"

"Not so funny kine den, Uncle. Smart."

I poured out another handful of peanuts for him. It was slimy and white with mold.

"Aw, this is no good Uncle," I shouted, excited and worried about the ones he had already eaten.

"It's too old Uncle, don't eat it," I said as I swept the rest off the table into the bag. He was quiet. Like a scolded child. I looked down at his feet and I recognized my mother's round script again: Kam Chong Lee written across both slippers in black felt pen. They reminded me of a boxful of little girl's slippers that I had just marked with my daughter's name in preparation for school. And it all finally seemed right somehow. All of it. Uncle Kam Chong and Palolo Home and his name written across his slippers and me writing my daughter Lisa's name on hers. And the long line of toothless Chinese men and women who lived here and those yet to come. I took my place in that line and glanced down at my slippers.

I left them just the way I found them. Uncle was sitting outside, cane in his lap. Mr. Chun was smoking. Mr. Tam was waving enthusiastically from the TV room. I waved back and grinned. I'd be back.

*****

The last time I saw Uncle at Palolo Home, he was in bed, sleeping. My mother went over called to him and shook him awake. He was much thinner than I had remembered him.

She asked him, "You know who this is?" pointing in my direction. He turned and looked at me, not really recognizing me until she prompted him, "That's Darrell."

He turned to me and muttered, "Ho, they treat you rough ova heah, you know. Not so easy ovah heah. Some of the new guys they treat um extra rough. But I don't say anyting. Bumbye dey learn. I donno why dey so rough."

My mother looked at me, then said to him, "Not everybody can get to be almost ninety, you know."

"Huh, not so easy being old," he grumbled. "I don't know if dey let me reach da two numbah." I didn't understand. I gave my mother a puzzled look.

"You know, when you get to ninety-one, you supposed to go church and pray. Ask if dey let you reach the two numbah...ninety-two. Plenny guys believe dat. Even if dey no go church. Hard to go church around heah." Next March was Uncle's birthday, ninetieth; ninety-one by the Chinese calendar. My mother reassured him, "You gonna make it. No worry. You rest."

"Not so much fun being sick. Not easy, you know!"

"You pretty good today. Your nose not so runny. When you get bettah, you be all right," my mother said. "They come and take you in the wheelchair to eat, huh? Later on you can walk again by yourself to the dining room."

"Who stay Nellie's house now? The other night, I went Nellie's house sleep. Den two guys come in. I donno dem," Uncle said.

"Calvin stay Nellie's house. He live there." My mother humored him; didn't correct his mistaken notion of an overnight stay away from Palolo Home. She looked up and smiled at me.

I *could* imagine Uncle spending the night at my long-dead aunt's. It was the house that Ah Po, my grandmother, lived in in her later years. I could see him in the kitchen with a cup of tea on the table. Or in the front room facing the street watching the traffic. I remembered that he went to Auntie Nellie's funeral, the last one he attended before he came to the Home. It was a big Chinese funeral. Lots of people came to see their *tsien tsang*, their teacher. Auntie Nellie had taught Chinese school for years. Probably taught them as she had taught me: behave yourself, take care your elders, serve them tea and maybe they'll give you a *lee see*, a coin wrapped in red paper. And never, *ever* miss a funeral or *bai sahn*, the annual visit to the cemetery to pay your respects to your ancestors. Even when I was in

178

my twenties she would praise me profusely for showing up at these occasions. No more quarters wrapped up in red paper but she still said, "Good boy. Good boy," as if I were nine. So it seemed okay that Uncle would "spend the night" at Auntie Nellie's house...

A round-faced man walked into the room, Uncle's roommate. He wore a long-sleeved shirt and blue slacks pulled way up over a neat pot belly. He carried a cane although he really didn't seem to need it. He looked at us wide-eyed, innocent and said, "I almost drowned this morning. Yeah, the water was up to here!" He indicated neck level with his palm.

"All kinda people was here. They just walk into da room. All kine...Hawaiians, grandchildren, little babies. They just walk in!"

"And this machine..." He pointed toward the wheelchair at the foot of Uncle's bed. "I donno who ordered dis. They wheel dis ting in. I donno who brought um. Ho, da water was high! Little more I needed a boat."

He moved over to his bed and tentatively pushed at the middle of the mattress. He looked up at us and confided, "I just testing to see if da water too deep..."

My mother and I smiled at him and tried not to pay too much attention as he continued his story. Uncle complained some more about the rough treatment. I asked to take his picture.

"Nah, I no like. Too much trouble get out of bed," he said.

"No, you can stay in bed," I said. "I no mo any pictures of you and your sistah." He sat up for two shots with my mother sitting next to the bed. I snuck a closeup of him before he slid back down under the covers. We were quiet for a while watching his eyes open and close.

"Da eye tired," my mother commented. "Da mind awake, but da eye tired."

I imagined that he was staying at Auntie Nellie's again or traveling somewhere else. No deep water or boats where Uncle was going.

The phone rang. It was my mother. "Dr. Wong just called. *Kau Goong*, Uncle, just passed away."

She said, "Daddy and I went to visit him yesterday. He was okay. He kept asking me when they were going to put him in the hospital. He wanted to go to the hospital. Good ting we went to see him yesterday." She laughed, "He asked for *hahm gnee*, salt fish. He wasn't eating anything, just kept getting shriveled up and skinnier. And he asked for *hahm gnee*."

The pictures of my mother and Uncle Kam Chong came back today from Long's Drugs. They're not particularly good pictures. My mother and uncle have matching liver spots on the sides of their faces. Uncle is bald and my mother's hair is mostly grey and thinning. There's no mistaking that they're related...

My mother has this old picture of my grandmother sitting in the middle of all her kids. All eight of them. Ah Po doesn't look much older than her eldest daughter. Everyone is in a stiff, formal pose. My mother's a little girl, maybe four or five, wearing a dress and a huge bow in her hair. Uncle Kam Chong looks around twenty. Ah Po is sitting in the middle of her brood, unsmiling. The wide Chinese-style headband across her forehead makes her look small-faced, her eyes dark and beady. She has a pale, clear complexion...

There's a picture at my folks' house of me and my brother with our parents. My mother looks young and pretty. We don't ever remember our mothers that way. She's very serious. And her skin is clear, unflawed. My father is in a suit, his hair slicked back with Dixie Peach pomade. My brother is standing next to him, his hair combed in the same way. I hardly had any hair but what little I had was slicked down flat. I must have been about one or two years old, sitting on Ma's lap with a finger in my mouth. My father always points out that I was quite a thumb-sucker. They say that my brother and I look alike. I never thought so before but looking at it now, there might be some resemblance...

Then there's the picture of me on my tricycle grimacing, heading full speed straight into the old Brownie. My brother must've taken that one. I wouldn't care if I ran him over. There's a picture of him with his shirt off showing off his left bicep and making "big chest." He has this tight grin on his face, as if it were making the muscle bigger.

The lower jaw tight, the neck tense, the same mouth pulled down at the corners. There's no mistaking that we're related. No mistaking.

J'like Ten Thousand   Darrell H.Y. Lum

My fahdah stay so tight, so pa-ke. He no like buy firecracker, man. He only buy one five hundred pack fo burn at New Year's time. Ho man, everybody get da thousands or da five thousand strings or even da ten thousand strings but Daddy, he no like buy nutting fo me. He only say, "Jes throw away money dat. One boom and pau. All day money go up in smoke. And da ting only make rubbish." He so tight. Every year, he buy only one five hundred pack fo burn, fo good luck. And he only buy me stuff like cracker balls or sparkalahs. And I only get one hundred pack sometimes or sometimes one pack of baby Camels, ass da real small firecrackers dat only make one soft pop, from Firecracker Uncle. Good ting I get Firecracker Uncle or I wouldn't get nutting fo burn.

Firecracker Uncle always get one Christmas party his house every year on da night befoa Christmas. His Christmas party da bes man, cause everytime he give firecracker to da kids. Kids not supposed to pop firecracker but he give us. He da Firecracker Uncle.

Everybody gotta eat dinner first. But everybody know what going get aftahwards so dey eat real fast and try figgah out where Firecracker Uncle going sit. Da small kids donno what going happen, so easy for get dem fo move from da good spots. Jes gotta tell, "Eh, dis my spot. You gotta move. Try look, you see dis mark on da floor, ass means dis my spot!"

When Auntie Sadie pass out da song sheets aftah everybody pau eat dat means pretty soon Firecracker Uncle going come. Of course everybody know we gotta sing da "Twelve Days of Christmas" Hawaiian style and Uncle Boo-boo everytime wave his beer when come to "ten can of bee-ya." And den we gotta sing "Jingle Bells" and right in da middle get Firecracker Uncle, I mean Santa Claus, ringing da doorbell. Auntie Sadie send da smallest kid fo go open da door. She throw da ack, she tell, "I wondah who dat?" Anyway, it only Firecracker Uncle. Can

182

tell cause when he give out da presents, Auntie gotta bring his glasses udderwise he no can read da tags. And Firecracker Uncle get gold teet and his hands always smell like fish from selling fish at da fish market, so gotta be him, yeah? He give out all da presents calling out our name one by one. Da small kids little bit scared but us big guys not scared. Jes gotta go, shake hands l'dat and he give you your present.

Dis da only Christmas present dat my muddah let me open befoa Christmas cause everybody else's muddah let da kids open. Dis time, inside da big kids present had one pack firecrackers, numbah one hundred kine, one pack sparkalahs, and one pack cracker balls.

Was funny cause aftah all da kids went open their presents, my muddah and everybody's muddah made all da kids go to uncle and tell him in Chinese, "Dough jay, Goo Geong." You know, fo say tank you to uncle. Was funny cause everybody went line up and say, "Tank you, Uncle" when he still yet was in his Santa Claus suit. Anyway, every year da big kids got firecracker from Firecracker Uncle. Of course da small kids only got sparkalahs and cracker balls. But if uncle gave you firecrackers, ass means you was old enough fo burn.

Aftah all dis was pau, we had to sing "Jingle Bells" again and when Firecracker Uncle came back in his regular clothes, he went try ack like wasn't him. But was, yeah?

When we went home, I wanted to open up my firecracker package but my muddah said I couldn't touch um until New Year's Eve.

Ho man, sometimes I stay tink about um though. I tink, how many get inside? I wondah if every one going pop. I start figgah-ing out where in da yard I goin pop um. Like by da mock orange hedge, where if you put one inside da middle, all da leaves fall down when you blass um. By da rock wall by where da toad live. By da witch lady's house. You gotta have all da spots ready you know, cause no mo dat much inside da pack, no can waste um. Ass why you gotta open up da pack of firecrackers and

unwind da string dat hold da pack together so dat you can burn um one by one. I jes wish sometimes I could have one pack dat I could jes burn all one time.
One ten thousand string, maybe.

New Year's Eve aftah I pau eat dinner, my muddah finally went tell I could go pop my firecrackers. You know, if you count da one hundred pack, no mo one hundred firecrackers inside, only get thirty seven. Ho, da gyp! My fahdah said dat da hundred pack supposed to mean dat it *sound* like one hundred explosions not dat it get one hundred firecrackers inside. I nevah believe. I jes told him, "I wish I had one ten thousand one. Would be sharp yeah? One long string, all popping wit sparks and fire all ovah..." My fahdah nevah say nutting. He was jes going be tight.

So aftah I went blass all of mines, I went go see if Brynie next door had anymoa. Sometimes he gimme some. Brynie's fahdah always buy him plenny packs. By da time we was pau wit our firecrackers and we went play cracker ball fight wit slingshot, Brynie's fahdah was ready fo pop his long strings. My fahdah came out of da house and even if he went say to Mama, "Mistah Kawamura going burn money again!" he came out to watch too. Sometimes Mistah Kawamura get five, mebbe six strings. Five thousands and one supah-long ten thousand fo da end. My fahdah, he no like buy but he like watch um pop. I tink he like some of da good luck come by him. Mistah Kawamura got out da laddah and went hang up da strings from da basketball net. He make us laugh, Mista Kawamura, cause he always get one cigarette in his mout while he stay hanging up da firecrackers. Everytime his cigarette come close to da firecrackers, me and Brynie, we jump back, man. Den when everyting ready, he check to make sure me and Brynie was on da porch and he wave to my Daddy and he take da cigarette out of his mout and light um. He just light um and den run away fast. He come by us fo watch.

I like da bomb part da bes. Das da las part of da string when get plenny firecrackers pop all at da same time. When Mistah Kawamura say we can, Brynie and me go look fo da ones dat nevah pop and save um so dat we can pop um bumbye.

Pretty soon only get smoke. Only can see Mistah Kawamura running through da smoke fo hang up one nudda string. Only can see his cigarette come bright jes befoa he light da string. Den only can see him running out from da smoke and den da bomb at da end. PRAAWK! I foget already how many strings he went pop dis time but was real plenny. I jes knew was pau when he went pop da ten thousand one.

Mama went tell Daddy dat midnight went pass already. Mama went light da punk fo burn our firecrackers and Daddy went get his five hundred pack. First he practice swing his hand couple times, fo practice where he going throw um. No can hang up da five hundred pack, too small dat. Daddy jes throw um. He went rip open da bottom jes little bit and pull out da fuses.

"Mama," he went wave his hand fo da punk and Mama gave him da punk and he went practice throw somemoa times. Me and Mama stay little bit back, kinda scary when Daddy getting ready fo throw. Daddy, he always light um and den he wait little bit, he no throw um right away. He wait until da ting is lighted good. Daddy went light um and den he went wait little bit. Me and Mama went move little mo back. Da stuff was spitting sparks and fire befoa he went throw um. And when he went throw um, was jes like one rocket. Da fuses was spitting sparkles and den while still yet was in da air, da firecrackers start fo pop. POP...POP...POP. Slow and den got faster. POP, POP, POP, POP. And den jes when hit da ground: PROPP, POP, POP. PRAAWK! Not too long da pops but was sharp still yet.

Den Daddy went signal Mama and tell, "Get da uddah one Mama." And Mama got one nuddah pack from inside da house. I thought only had one pack but Daddy had one nudda one. He went look at me and tell me, "You like pop um?"

I wasn't too sure but he jes went tell me, "Hea, come o'hea." And he went gimme da firecrackers. Den he went show me how you can tell which side fo open, da side dat get da fuses. Den he hold my hand and we went practice throw.

"Swing la dis," he went tell me and he swing his hand holding my hand and I can see da firecracker pack flying awready wit da sparks and da fire shooting from da fuse part. Like one rocket.

"You going help me eh, Daddy?" I went ask him.

"No worry. No worry." And we went practice again. And again. And den he went say, "We ready, Mama." Mama went gimme da punk. And Daddy and me went line up, me in front, Daddy in back. His hands was big on top mines: punk hand and firecracker hand.

"You ready?" I only stay looking down at da punk and da five hundred pack and Daddy's hand went put da punk by da firecracker fuse. I wanted fo throw awready but Daddy's hand was holding me back. I like throw. I like throw! And den I went jes look at da fuse and da punk and it was jes starting fo light. Jes little bit. And was j'like I went throw um already I could see da sparks and da fire and da pops in da air.

And den it went catch good. Was spitting sparks anykine way. And my hand wasn't fighting Daddy's anymoa and we went throw da firecrackers da same way we went practice and da stuff was spitting sparks and fire in da air. Like one rocket. And while was still in da air, it started fo pop: POP, POP, POP, PRAAWK! Daddy's hand went let go mines.

Was only five hundred, but Daddy and me, we went pop um j'like was ten thousand.

186

Chinese Fireworks
Banned in Hawaii
for Uncle Wongie, 1987

Eric Chock

Almost midnight, and the aunties
are wiping the dinner dishes
back to their shelves,
cousins eat jook from the huge vat
in the kitchen, and small fingers
help to mix the clicking ocean
of mah jong tiles, so the uncles can play
through another round of seasons.
And you put down your whiskey
and go outside to find your long bamboo pole
so Uncle Al can help you tie on
a ten foot string of good luck,
red as the raw fish we want
on our plates every New Year's.
As you hang this fish over the railing
Uncle Al walks down the steps
and with his cigarette lighter
ignites it and jumps out of the way
as you lean back and jam the pole
into the bottom of your guts,
waving it across the sky,
whipping sparks of light from its tail,
your face in a laughing Buddha smile
as you trace your name in the stars
the way we teach our kids to do
with their sparklers.
This is the family picture
that never gets taken, everyone
drawn from dishes and food and games
and frozen at the sound
of 10,000 wishes filling our bodies
and sparkling our eyes.
You play the fish till its head explodes
into a silence that echoes,

scattering red scales to remind us of spirits
that live with us in Hawaii.
Then, as we clap and cheer,
the collected smoke of our consciousness
floats over Honolulu, as it has
each year for the last century.
But tonight, as we leave,
Ghislaine stuffs her styrofoam tea cup
full of red paper from the ground.
This is going to be history, she says.
Let's take some home.

Looking Back from a Small Hill to Downtown Honolulu — Eric Chock

An old dirt road connected our homes
with a medial strip of blackened weeds
that each of our families greased in common
tickling the underbellies of our primitive machines.
Pa drove our jalopy jeep slow
to savor each bump, making me
start wishing at a young age
for a thicker cushion that wouldn't
slide back and forth across the metal seat,
though with each kick from below
I would rise, for an instant, tall enough
to see ahead through the windshield
to where weeds ended in a road paved
totally with black oil, greased so smooth
I could see how easy it would be for us
to get to that ocean that, from here,
seemed ready to spill
into downtown Honolulu.

But Pa always knew better. That water
sparkled with circular rainbows that leaked
from ships, through the harbor, each claiming
entry into the heart of Hawaii's commerce.
So Pa turned our backs on the town
and drove us across the snake that wriggles
over the Pali. The road must have lived then,
its dotted white backbone almost hidden
by giant hanging philodendron vines,
elephant ears in the trees,
and at the meanest turns the wiggly arrow
"snake signs" he told us they were.
They say there were no snakes in Hawaii then.
Not even in the zoo in Waikiki.
But knowing they existed elsewhere
in the world, we headed for the country,

189

found dirt roads to beaches of the windward side,
and waited for someone to hook by mistake
a pale blue-skinned "white eel"
which swallows the baited hook whole
and ties its body in knots of panic
tangling the lines. Pretending snake,
we'd tease and torture the eel
with knives and spears when it landed.
All dead eels stink. White eels at least
you can give to the old Japanese men to eat.
But if none of the few who knew how
wanted to trouble themselves with all the
skinning, cleaning, the preparation to make it
into a suitable meal, we'd kill it
there in the sand, and leave it for
the crabs, and waves, or maybe for
some poor fisherman to strip into bait.

Riding back at the widening end of one of those days,
the jeep grinding through the sand and tall weeds
bouncing me and the fishing gear to my last
backward glimpse of the open sea,
the long bamboo poles strapped but jiggling
alongside the jalopy, sometimes I'd pretend
I was a foot soldier in World War II
claiming the beach, for our side, for Hawaii.
We hadn't lost it then,
and could drive the black snake home
up the dirt weed road to the homestead.
Above the harbor full of ships
I washed off the knives and spears and poles
with fresh water.

The Mango Tree   Eric Chock

"One old Chinese man told me," he said, "that he like to trim his tree so the thing is hollow like one umbrella, and the mangoes all stay hanging underneath. Then you can see where all the mangoes stay, and you know if ripe. If the branches stay growing all over the place, then no can see the mango, and the thing get ripe, and fall on da ground."

And us guys, we no eat mango that fall down. Going get soft spots. And always get plenty, so can be choosy. But sometimes, by the end of mango season when hardly get already, and sometimes the wind blow 'em down, my mother, sometimes she put the fall down kind in the house with the others.

I was thinking about that as I was climbing up the tree. The wind was coming down from the pali, and I gotta lean into the wind every time she blow hard. My feet get the tingles cause sometimes the thing slip when I try for grip the bark with my toes. How long I never go up the tree! I stay scared the branch going broke cause too small for hold me, and when the wind blow, just like being on one see-saw. And when I start sawing that branch he told me for cut, the thing start for jerk, and hard for hold on with my feet. Plus I holding on to one branch over my head with one hand, and the fingers getting all cramp. My legs getting stiff and every few strokes my sawing arm all tired already, so when the wind blow strong again, I rest. I ride the branch just like one wave. One time when I wen' look down I saw him with one big smile on his face. Can tell he trying hard not for laugh.

He getting old but he spend plenty time in that tree. Sometimes he climb up for cut one branch and he stay up for one hour, just looking around, figuring out the shape of the tree, what branches for cut and what not for cut. And from up there can see the whole valley. Can see the trees and the blue mountains. I used to have nightmares that the thing was going erupt and flood us out with lava, and I used to run around looking for my girlfriend so she could go with us in our '50 Dodge when we run away to the ocean. But I never did find her and I got lost. Only could see smoke, and people screaming, and the lava coming down.

The nightmare every time end the same. I stay trapped on one trail in the mountains, right on one cliff. Me and some guys. The trail was narrow so we walking single file. Some people carrying stuff, and my mother in front of me, she carrying some things wrapped in one cloth. One time she slip, and I grab for her, and she starting to fall and I scream "Oh no!" and then I wake up. And I look out my window at the mango tree and the blue mountains up the valley. The first time I wen' dream this dream I was nine.

Since that time I wen dream plenty guys falling off the trail. And plenty times I wen grab for my mother's hand when she start for fall. But I never fall. I still stay lost on the cliff with the other guys. I still alive.

And my father still sitting in the mango tree just like one lookout, watching for me and my mother to come walking out of the mountains. Or maybe he stay listening to the pali wind for the sound one lady make if she fall. Or maybe he just sitting in his mango tree umbrella, rocking like one baby in the breeze, getting ripe where we can see him. And he making sure no more extra branches getting in his way.

Poem for My Father

Eric Chock

I lie dreaming
when my father comes to me and says,
I hope you write a book someday.
He thinks I waste my time,
but outside, he spends hours over stones,
gauging the size and shape a rock will take
to fill a space,
to make a wall of dreams around our home.
In the house he built with his own hands
I wish for the lure that catches all fish
or girls with hair like long moss in the river.
His thoughts are just as far and old
as the lava chips like flint off the hammer,
and he sees the mold of dreams
taking shape in his hands.
His eyes see across orchids on the wall,
into black rock, down to the sea,
and he remembers the harbor full of fish,
orchids in the hair of women thirty years before
he thought of me, this home, these stone walls.
Some rocks fit perfectly, slipping into place
with light taps of his hammer.
He thinks of me inside
and takes a big slice of stone,
and pounds it into the ground
to make the corner of the wall.
I cannot wake until I bring
the fish and the girl home.

Chinese New Year   Eric Chock

koong koong lights ten thousand wishes
he laughs at his grey hand
bursting into sparks

he takes two steps back
mosquito punk in hand

hard of hearing
he feels firecrackers
vibrating in his heart

red leaves cover his feet

What? Another Chinese Holiday?! Eric Chock

Moon Festival again,
black sugar cakes ruined
with old egg yolks.

No fireworks to
blow me away.
No lion dancing.

Just some folks
hyping old ways
to make a buck.

Who cares what
harvest the moon
shines on?

Where's a tv?
I wanna watch
the World Series!

Full moon?!
I don't even know
when it is.

If it's round
and white
in the October sky

it's gotta be
a home run,
cracking the American

night.

Fever
for Mona

Laureen Ching

Women are partnered
from the first with fire.
Prometheus did not steal it
no matter what the textbooks say
but a woman, nameless and quick.
Cornered, she swallowed.
Ate up the fire.
Afterward, it burned in her belly
like a wound heavy and deep.

She did not simply
keep the flame
she passed it on
daughter by daughter.
Each one possessing
the pit
the fire
her promise.
Scrape out your bones
for kindling if you must.
Turn flesh to flint.
Whatever is, is.
You burn for a reason.

A Pale Arrangement of Hands   Cathy Song

It has been raining all night
and into the morning.
I sit, listening to the rain,
my hands on the kitchen table.
Their knuckles, yellow white
like the tendons of a drumstick,
the skin pulled taut to make a fist.
I remember my mother's hands,
how nervous they always seemed
except when they were busy cooking.
Her hands would assume a certain confidence
then, as she rubbed and patted butter
all over a turkey as though
she were soaping and scrubbing up a baby.

I wonder what she would prescribe
in weather like this. In Wahiawa,
it rained even when the sun was shining
through the mock orange trees.
"Liquid sunshine," she used to say
to the three of us peering from the jalousies
as if it happened only here,
in this part of the world.
The rain fell like a fence around our house,
in big drops slapping the mud
with the sound of slippers approaching,
housewives from the neighborhood
shaking their umbrellas at the kitchen door.

We sat in rapt attention
as Mother served her girl friends
instant coffee and caramel candy.
We knew the mothers by their children:
the mother of the boy who had ringworm;
the mother of the girl with the eleven cavities.
Ours was the youngest mother—slender,

with a bright red flower mouth,
being partial to Calypso Coral
sold at the Kress makeup counter.
I liked to watch her apply the lipstick:
first, she would stretch her lips
back into a wide square smile,
smear on the waxy color
and then with a soundless smack,
she would leave her mouthprint
on some white tissue.
I think she was pleased
the day she discovered something else
for us to do on those rainy afternoons:
showing us how to make artificial carnations
out of those discarded tissues
with a couple of hairpins.

Down the hall in the end room
she shared with our father,
she let us watch an hour of cartoons;
allowing herself time to fix
the tuna casserole or the Vienna sausages.
We were permitted to drift through the house,
within its safe circumference,
its comfortable geography.
If we became restless,
the sandbox in the covered patio
was the farthest distance we could travel,
stopping short of the rain.

We were three mild lunatics
she found herself with each day
in a chicken-coop house:
one child singing to herself,
a crinoline worn on her head like a shroud;
another bringing gifts of wildlife,
mongoose and centipedes;
and the youngest, a boy who sat
pugnaciously in front of the dryer,

watching his flannel blanket swirl clean,
refusing to go anywhere without it.

For my mother,
the afternoons brought
the longest part of the day.
I remember the frustrated look
when we refused to nap;
if only we would close our eyes,
be good, try to sleep.
I have no children but as I sit here
with my hands on my lap
and the rain falling outside the window,
I realize what power we wielded
when we were young.
Sleep meant pretending. Lying still
but alert, I listened from the next room
as my mother slipped out of her damp dress.
The cloth crumpling onto the bathroom floor
made a light, sad sound.

Living Near the Water   Cathy Song

He lived near the water
most of his life
which gave him the smell of the sea.
His body had grown furry
with a soft blue gray covering of hair.
His bare feet seemed rooted to the grass
where the toenails had thickened
into the ebony shell of snails.
In his lawn chair, he appeared
mammoth and prehistoric.

The day before he died,
we were sitting beside him in the yard.
The day was clear and ending and
we could feel the presence of water
as if waves were boiling right off shore.
There was the odor of salt burning,
of some drowsy spice between the trees.
The radio was on,
the dial set fuzzily between two channels.
He had been listening to the static
as though he were waiting to decipher
a message he would know
at the moment of his hearing it.
The tiny hairs in his ears, insectlike,
registering an imperceptible music.
In his right hand he held a flyswatter
which he waved like a wand
in between his moments of rest.
Those moments were lengthening
like the equatorial light of summer.
The children squirmed. The mosquitoes
had gone to rest beneath the leaves.

Still and distant,
he contained great mystery.

His clotted eye had seen
a world transformed by fire—
the stooped soldiers offering
a young boy strips of shredded meat
alongside the burning trees;
the night his son gently shook him
from sleep to witness
the astronauts somersaulting on the moon.
And in the pinpoint blue of his iris,
like snow falling inside a paperweight,
was the day his young man's eyes had scanned
the cargo of brides
who bowed before the grim life held out to them;
sucking in their breath
at the vision of their own faces
caught like orange blossoms
in the sad hands of laborers.
Those of us assembled on that day
had descended from that moment of regret;
my grandmother stepping forward
to acknowledge her own face
was the last to give herself away.

He was tired.
He had traveled in silence
since the day her eyes had fallen
upon his ill-fitting suit, his borrowed shoes.
From that moment she gave everything away.
He had traveled so long in silence
that when he turned and said,
"I love you" to my father
who was holding the youngest red-faced child,
he had clicked off the radio,
he was saying goodbye.
And then he grew thirsty,
having carried that stone on his tongue
that he moved to reach for his water.
I watched my father
bring the cup to his father's mouth, watched

how it was the son's hand that trembled.
The children were put to sleep
and while we dreamed, my father
was still holding the hand long after
the warm wind had passed through him;
flowing out through each of us,
the smell of the sea.

Shadow Figures

1.
For a few moments in history
we were close, like twins
whispering without lights,
telepathic.
you in the top bunk,
your slight body
wheezing in the wind
stirring pollen.
We listened for the dog's
scratching on the screen,
etching metallic messages
with a deliberate paw.
The pink calloused skin
padded to our corner of the house,
his collar bell jingling
like money in the pocket.

Fifteen years later,
another boy walks out of the house.
He is selling a litter of kittens.
I hold one,
feeling the delicate bones
curl in my hand.
My father and three Tongans
built this wall,
I will never tell this boy
with peach colored hair.
And the bougainvillea they transplanted
from a seedling has grown
extravagant with age,
spilling a waterfall of blossoms,
purple and fuchsia.
I see the matchstick house,
riddled with termites,
had a luxuriance

my brother and I imagined.
But the sense of refuge was real.

2.
In similar weather,
mist pressing close to earth,
there is a stillness
to the afternoon I remember
in Golden Gate Park
when we were very young.
My brother was feeding rice
crackers to the squirrels
nibbling their way to his hand
laid on the grass,
still and unafraid.
He was small and smooth,
calm as a stone in a garden,
full and oval in its contemplation
as if all of its life
it had absorbed the sound of rain.
We called my brother Mahatma Gandhi
because he was thin and dark.
We called him Gandhi
for the eggplant hue of his slight body
against the pale soles of his feet.

This was before
we moved into adolescence
and into separate rooms.
When you were no longer here
but buried beneath
a quilt of comics,
wearing headsets that made
you look like an insect.
On Saturdays I knew
where to find you—
knees bent, stroking
the chalky fur of the terrier
whose tongue flicked

like a pink ribbon.
He seemed content to wait
at your side, forever
if you had wished,
for the soggy tennis ball
to be thrown one last time
across the yard.

3.
"Look how he loves us!"
we said
as the dog humped our legs.
He had the yard,
the pool (his water dish),
the cool dirt beneath the trees.
Then days when he saw no one
but our mother hanging the morning wash.

High-strung,
heartflutter of a hummingbird,
he longed for the great escape.
He jumped out of our arms
and missed the gate;
misjudged the shrub's height.
A slipped disk and
a chicken wire barricade
reinforced his persistence.
He was bold about his intentions:
dug a mine field of trenches
in the back yard.
He was forty-nine in dog years,
and old man,
by the time he finally made it,
tunneling across to the other side.
After a week,
he returned scruffy and beat.

4.
He died a year later.

One day after school
we turned the corner to find
the gate unlatched,
swinging open like a gaping jaw.
We flung our books
and ran into the silent yard,
the spool of dread unwinding
as though we were held
pinned under water.
The blood hammered in my throat.
The shelter of years we built
had sapped his instinct.
When the neighbor's sheep dog
clamped its teeth,
it was a bear trap
locking rust and death
around the hind leg of a rabbit.

I heard your voice that night
like a high pitched frequency
call his name,
your body poised like an antenna
on top of the jungle gym.
Twelve years old,
your body a flag of grief.

We lived in that house
for many years.
But after the death,
I never knew
what came to replace for you
that small intelligent animal.
His quick ears picking out
the pulse of your sleep.
In this life,
this is what we have—
the two of us
in the interval we call childhood—
shadow figures in a matchstick house.

The Tower of Pisa   Cathy Song

There was always something that needed fixing,
a car on the blink,
a jinxed washing machine,
a high-strung garbage disposer.
His life was one of continual repair.
He toyed with gadgets,
made them hum, churn, spin.
And when, miraculously, nothing needed him,
he set his tinkering soul onto larger schemes:
major home improvements.
He built courtyards and patios,
innumerable extensions,
doubling the size of the original bungalow,
planted olive trees outside my window.
The lattice-work of grapevines,
the frothy bougainvilleas
were his ideas: to cultivate an oasis
on a suburban street.
He didn't mind the physical work,
he was glad for it.
For a living, he spent his days
strapped inside a cockpit,
shuttling tourists from one island to another,
with not even a tsunami
to relieve the monotony of a routine
take-off, a routine three-point landing.
Never a cloud in that tropical sky,
nothing so much as a stray nene bird on the runway
to test his ability.
A boy who wanted nothing else
but to fly those gorgeous machines.
It was maddening, the inactivity,
the call to mediocrity. Any idiot,
he insisted, can sit and steer on automatic pilot.
Those were the days he chomped furiously
on big cigars and snacksize Hershey bars.

So weekends found him scrunched on the kitchen floor
amid a chaos of nuts and bolts and screws,
with no manual to guide him—
a Chinese torture puzzle to me,
sweet labor to him.
Or hammering as if his life depended on it,
his mouth bristling with nails.
I'd get dizzy watching him at that great height,
on top a rickety, paint-splattered ladder,
swaying like the Tower of Pisa.
I was always afraid he'd hurt himself,
die and leave us unprepared.
When I was six, I witnessed
a pickax slam into his right hand,
how with a sharp intake of breath—
he made no other sound—
he reversed the action, the miscalculation,
in grueling slow motion.
I knew he needed protecting.
I was convinced of it.
From that moment, I became his shadow,
a pair of eyes on the lookout
for imminent catastrophe,
scanning the yard for possible pitfalls—
removing shovels, nails, bear-clawed weeders
from his path,
anchoring the flimsy ladder as he descended,
gropingly, paint or sawdust in his eyes.
I was never far from his ferocious energy.
On my bicycle I'd patrol the patio and the pool,
anticipating any threat of danger.
He thought I had nothing better to do—
How could he interpret my devotion?—
and he'd send me on errands
which would worry me,
leave him unguarded.
He'd call me Speedy Gonzalez
when I'd bring, in record time, iced tea,

cloudy with saccharine the way he liked it.
See? I'd tell myself, nothing happened.
I went, was gone, he's still here,
alive, sprinkled with sawdust,
thirsty, a man of forty-five.
A year later he suffered a myocardial infarction.
He was flying between two islands
when, like a piece of shrapnel, the pain hit.
When he landed, he drove himself to the hospital.

What makes a child sense a parent's fragility?
What I had seen years ago had been dramatic enough:
the gashed hand brimming with blood.
But it seems gentler than that,
a kind of eavesdropping,
when I saw in my father someone else
a man who, night after night,
after he thought we were asleep,
would play the same recording of *La Bohème*,
softly so as not to wake us,
and go out into the yard.
I listened as the music
flowed through my room
on its way toward him,
sitting on a lawn chair in the dark,
poised to receive the perfect pitch,
each aria projecting him somewhere I could not reach:
stunned at my body's resistance to make music.
The flat refusal.

It was the striving for perfection,
wasn't it,
and the falling short
that made him return each night
to the one source of beauty that consoled him,
the untiring devotion of the human soul,
distilled in the purest vibrato
that sings undiminished,
unhampered there above the trees.

And he could weep because of it,
because he thought he was alone.

He says I saved my own life
that day I fell into the pool.
I'm not so sure.
I was riding my bicycle
with one eye on him
when I toppled in.
I hadn't yet learned to swim.
I would've stayed at the bottom—
for a second, I was resigned to it—
where it not for his arm reaching out
like a branch above the water.
I owed him this
all my life—this worry,
this constant concern.
I was his shadow,
a child trying to make sense of it all,
hinged on disaster,
a child waiting for my father to fall.

Heaven   Cathy Song

He thinks when we die we'll go to China.
Think of it—a Chinese heaven
where, except for his blond hair,
the part that belongs to his father,
everyone will look like him.
China, that blue flower on the map,
bluer than the sea
his hand must span like a bridge
to reach it.
An octave away.

I've never seen it.
It's as if I can't sing that far.
But look—
on the map, this black dot.
Here is where we live,
on the pancake plains
just east of the Rockies,
on the other side of the clouds.
A mile above the sea,
the air is so thin, you can starve on it.
No bamboo trees
but the alpine equivalent,
reedy aspen with light, fluttering leaves.
Did a boy in Guangzhou dream of this
as his last stop?

I've heard the trains at night
whistling past our yards,
what we've come to own,
the broken fences, the whiny dog, the rattletrap cars.
It's still the wild west,
mean and grubby,
the shootouts and fistfights in the back alley.
With my son the dreamer
and my daughter, who is too young to walk,

I've sat in this spot
and wondered why here?
Why in this short life,
this town, this creek they call a river?

He had never planned to stay,
the boy who helped to build
the railroads for a dollar a day.
He had always meant to go back.
When did he finally know
that each mile of track led him further away,
that he would die in his sleep,
dispossessed,
having seen Gold Mountain,
the icy wind tunneling through it,
these landlocked, makeshift ghost towns?

It must be in the blood,
this notion of returning.
It skipped two generations, lay fallow,
the garden an unmarked grave.
On a spring sweater day
it's as if we remember him.
I call to the children.
We can see the mountains
shimmering blue above the air.
If you look really hard
says my son the dreamer,
leaning out from the laundry's rigging,
the work shirts fluttering like sails,
you can see all the way to heaven.

Immaculate Lives

Cathy Song

We long for the quiet
domesticity of those Dutch interiors,
the girl at the window,
head bent over a piece of sewing
so that the light
saturating the deft plaits
would take our breath away.
They were right.
In praise of light,
they gave us hair,
the honey yellows,
terrains of ocher, mustard, amber
to offset the rational tiles,
the black and white squares
laid as if for a game of chess,
the courtly pattern in which they moved,
restrained, knowing the intricate rules.
A flood of letters never cluttered the table.
A pitcher of milk, a simple meal
could trigger a sumptuous
feast of architecture and light.
They savored what they knew,
intelligence and discipline
bearing fruit in domestic discovery—
the mirror a velvet lake.
If they chose to speak,
they did so expensively,
each word the weight of gold
coins in exchange for silence.
The heavy clink of meaning.
We could learn such thrift.
A flurry of papers like insects swarm our doorsteps.
We waste a thousand words
and still have not said it,
or said it a thousand times.
They have cleaned their houses for us,

swept and tidied the kitchen,
hid the pail of slop from view.
We move like pawns toward checkmate—
the pristine corner
chiseled by the diamond light
and the dazzling dexterity of our hosts,
the lacemaker, the glassblower—
stunned at the immaculate lives
we are unable to keep.

Pa-ke

Herbert K.K. Chun

you speak of shadows
and I dream of journeys—

an old ship, iron and rusted
plates. Chinese workers for sugar
plantations. I move among
broken sandals and jade-
colored bile. once a week,
they wash the hold. the water
slides across the deck, over yellow
bodies. it clings to the rusted hull.

from the vats
of cooking rice, the steam
rises in the twilight. we gather
near the warmth with our wooden
bowls. the brown rice
is over-cooked. burnt rice
scraped for those at the end
of the line. someone says every man
who can walk off the ship in Hawai'i
is worth five
dollars. there are no more
men, only hollow trees. hunger,
a sparrow, flutters
among the branching bones, taking each
grain of rice. it sings and its voice
enchants the twilight
into a shadowed sigh.

Ling Wan has died. I helped
throw him into the sea. his
feet were cold and stiff. his
toenails were black. I wear his
sandals. I keep his last
words. they are,

"do not let me die."

the island, a broken piece
of jade, rises with the dawn.
and the deck is full of wandering
eyes. behind me is
Fan Wei, whose sickness covers
him with sweat, as though
he had been
laboring instead of eating
rats. gone is the pain
in my legs, where the skin
is raw from scratching at sores
as I slept. now we smile
into each other's faces. soon,
soon...

I push my way off the ship.
I do not limp but walk
onto the dock. a man passes
and taps me on the shoulder
with a stick. I am
number nine. I throw my bowl
into the sea. too soon
I have need for another.

the night on this island
also sighs. I have journeyed far,
thinking that I had left
nothing behind.

Getting Groceries

Susan Lee St. John

On Saturdays we drive
our red Chevy
to Maunakea St.
Chinatown.

First the herbalist
in his dark room
Rows of drawers
filled with crumbling plants
lizard bile
desiccated bat eyes
wanting water for rebirth.
His brass balance
tarnished and still
in the stagnant air.

Three dirty old men
sit on a sidewalk bench
One pretends to read
a Chinese newspaper.

Don't look at them
my sister whispers.
They'll spit on you.
Hurry up, mama says.
We walk on the far edge
looking straight ahead.

Fermented duck eggs
fuzzy winter melon, gingko nuts
salted black beans
Let's have hamburger,
I say.
Shut up, mama says.

At Young's Noodle Factory

young women, gleaming with sweat,
swirl a white batter
over metal sheets,
shove them in a huge steamer.
We buy jee cheong fun:
glistening layers, folded
and wrapped
in butcher paper.
Across the street
a flashing marquee.
BOYS WILL BE GIRLS REVUE.

Mahus, mama says
under her breath.
One waves an emerald silk
handkerchief at us
Another in gold brocade
pouts full red lips.
I watch mama's face.
Be quiet and keep walking
she says.

John S.W. Lee

Susan Lee St. John

Li Sau Wong my father's name
Strong gold lion born
of magistrate and concubine.
She fed her child
chutney spiced with ginger.
Turquoise-silver brocade
tiny with exquisite frogs, fastened round
his soft white belly.
Sau Wong gurgled up brown sugar allspice;
his mother licked him clean.

At the Honolulu Shipyard everyone called him John or
Johnny. He signed his name John S.W. Lee. His home
phone rang for strangers: the "John Lee who works at the
Sears Automotive," or this or that John Lee. In the Oahu
phone book there were two-and-a-half pages of John
Lee's. John C.S. Lee, John H.L. Lee, John W.T. Lee...an
army of thin Chinese men in Bermuda shorts, made
indistinguishable by their adopted name.

Rice Cookers   Dana Leilehua Yuen

Some spirit stole rice cookers from our house.

Wedding anniversary rice cooker
or
Mother's Day rice cooker
It would not last long
often gone
before the first use.

I asked my grandmother
What happens to the rice cookers
Ah
You cannot burn
a crispy layer of rice for Grandfather to eat
in the bottom of a rice cooker.

Digging for
Lotus Roots   Kathleen Ngit Jun Young

Lotus roots grow deep in the mud. They are delicate, and break easily in harvesting. However, they are also light, and float to the surface when the soil above is cleared away.

I.

I was never sure if it was patience or a slowness of mind, but my father was the only one who could tame the wild kittens occasionally birthed under our house. He'd put food in the frying pan he'd found on the side of the road leading to Mosquito Junction, usually cut-up tilapia or sting ray, then he'd sit in the garage, about 5 feet away, and make his fishing lines, tying the hooks with his "special" knot, not seeming to pay any attention to the wild kittens, who, because of the smell maybe, or the sound of buzzing flies, were creeping out from under the house, heading cautiously towards the frying pan.

II.

"How do you let your children know that they've done something you disapprove of?"

The psychologist scrutinizes Mr. Wong, searching for any sign of connection. Mr. Wong, in turn, holds his face blank, and steady.

"I just no say nothing and they should get the idea."
Matter-of-factly.

"But how are they supposed to know what they've done, if you don't say anything?"

—pushing, always pushing, these haole birds think they know it all—

Mr. Wong closes his mouth in a tight line and makes no answer. She should get the idea.

Silence. Mrs. Wong is uncomfortable and wants to say something—anything. She glances at her daughter, staring out the window and blinking, at her husband, shut away now, and at the psychologist, writing the family problems down on a yellow pad.

"How much are we paying an hour?" Mrs. Wong asks, looking long and hard at her husband.

III.

There are two figures made with colored tissue paper standing in front of the coffin. They are the servants, there to make the transition into heaven easier. The *nam mo* is chanting and hitting the gong arrhythmically, calling out the names of the children "Kam Jin, Kam Chew, Kam Loy, Kam Ngao, Kam Kwai..." in tones rising and falling.

Time to get up again and circle the coffin. I don't know why my father does not lead the line. He's the oldest. But my Uncle Jimmy goes first, the firstborn of Popo's second marriage. If this bothers my father he doesn't show it. Same flat impassive face. Solemn as his only suit, a dark blue for many occasions.

We place paper money across Popo's body, single layers of gilt paper, some green paper in case heaven's currency is no longer gold, then gather it up to burn. My mother motions for me to stay next to the coffin and continue laying the paper out. I try not to imagine what I'd do if a bug crawled up my arm. I watch the smoke billow up to be caught by the white, vaulted ceiling. This funeral parlor really wasn't built for all this burning and gong chanting. The cemetery outside is filled with bodies placed in different directions: the *yup pun chai* lie with their feet towards the mountains, while Popo will have her head towards the hills, feet to the sea, like the rest of the Chinese buried there.

I've already determined, with a quick glance, that Popo looks very nice, peaceful, her face lightly powdered, jade earrings in her ears, a pearl between her lips to light the way. I don't think about the pearl, the darkness of death to be lit in an imaginary, or at least unknown, journey. If I must look at her, I look at the jade. I've never seen those earrings before.

222

IV.

The house stood on stilts next to the stream. Mud
flats of lotus began a few yards from the front steps. The
floor of the house was in constant need of repair, as the
boards damply rotted away, exposing the wet ground
below. On the dry slope in back, the chickens kicked up
dust, half wild but roosting in the scrap metal hen house.

Yook Fa lived in this house in defiance of her
mother. Three miles down the road, her mother owned
acres upon acres of rice. Ah Yook had four young ones
with a fifth on the way. It was getting hard to carry water
up the rickety stairs into the house, and there had been no
eggs laid for six days. She had sent the oldest out back to
look for nests among the haole koa, just in case. Her
oldest was seven, and the image of his father. Serious,
brooding, with a blunt tongue and a slow fuse, just like
his father, her dead husband, the one her mother had
never wanted her to marry because he was too old and
owned only a lotus farm.

Kam Ngao knew that he wouldn't find any eggs at
this time of day. It was past noon, and if the rats hadn't
gotten to the eggs, the mongoose would have. Kam Ngao
squatted in the shade of the hen house to think. He
wondered what mongoose tasted like. Probably better than
crayfish—more meat. Kam Ngao wanted to set a trap, like
the old man next door had taught him. All he needed was
a box and some string. Kwai was good at asking people
for things. Kwai was probably with the old man right now,
eating milk candy.

"Ngao! Eh! Try look what I got!" Kwai came scuttling
down the hill, something clenched in his hand, his eyes
round and bright.

"Lemme see. He wen give you candy?" Kam Ngao
asked, prying the object out of Kwai's fingers. It was a
clam shell. "So?"

"Come, come, we go to da pump," Kwai whispered,
giggling. "I show you."

Kwai led the way to their swimming hole. Lying on
his stomach and motioning his brother to do likewise, he

looked into the shallow water, where mosquito fish were swimming among the ung choi.

"Watch dis."

Inside the clam shell was a dark brown, waxy substance. With a reed, Kwai scooped out a lump and dropped it into the water.

"So?" demanded Ngao, tired of his brother's secrecy and thinking again about the mongoose trap.

"Try look da fishes," pointed Kwai.

Some guppies were attacking the brown lump furiously. The others were swimming around erratically, almost spasmodically.

"Api in," Ngao said, gulping. "That old man sells opium."

V.

There's a photograph of my father and I that has no place in my memory. It's of my father holding my hand as we walk along the pier at L-dock.

The thing is, I do remember going fishing with my father: I remember that we used to wake up at five o'clock in the morning in order to catch the ferry to Ford Island; I remember throwing crab nets off L-dock, thankful to get rid of the stink of the hammerhead bait; I remember being cut by the gill of the omaka as I was trying to get the hook out of its mouth; I remember afternoons of combing the shore near the dock, stones and broken shells crunching under my slippers, looking for the unusual...What I don't remember is my father ever holding my hand. I guess he must have, when I was small. I just don't remember.

VI.

"I can't see the boxes, how do you expect me to park between them?!"

It was three-thirty in the afternoon, and my father was trying to teach me how to parallel park.

"Okay, see dis can? I going put 'em right on da corna' of da box. Now you can see 'em?" My father stood next to the box and waited.

"Big help," I muttered, putting the car in reverse.

"Turn da wheel, turn the wheel! Da adda way!" he ordered.

The coke can fell off the box with a clatter.

"I can barely see the can! How do you expect me to do this?" It was hot and we had been doing this over and over for days.

"Concentrate," my father said. I noticed that he never seemed to sweat. "Make up your mind to do it."

VII.

"I needed one pencil. I neva have nothing." Kam Ngao's gaze was direct and unflinching. He only spoke English to his mother now, so she could learn.

"Why didn't you tell the teacher, like Kwai did?" Ah Yook said sharply in Chinese. She did not meet her son's dark eyes.

"I not Kwai. You wen send me school with nothing, just one white shirt on my back, das all." Ngao turned to look at the mud flats. "Da school said fo' us come early an' get cod liva oil an' poi. Dey no like us get malnutrition."

Kwai turned his back to his mother to change. His dark skin stretched taut, outlining his spine and ribs. He knew he was skinny, but he also knew he was strong. And he could harvest lotus roots without breaking the tubers.

VIII.

When my parents went to China for the first time, Popo asked my father to burn incense for her when he saw the statue of the great Buddha. Popo had been born in Hawaii and had never been to the homeland. And by that time she was too old to make the journey.

My father burned incense and made donations at every temple they visited. At Tunhuang, while visiting the Mogao caves he climbed the cliffs alone so he could circumambulate the huge Buddha there. He circled it twice.

When the typhoon hit Shanghai, my parent's tour

group missed it, having left the city just the day before. After that everyone on the tour burned incense at the temples.

IX.

Somehow our neighbor, who worked for a veterinarian, had heard that I'd wanted a kitten. I think my father had told her, in not so many words, that a kitten might take my mind off my mainland college failure. I left home shortly thereafter; nevertheless, our neighbor brought over an abandoned kitten.

According to my mother, the kitten looked like a wet, black rat, except that it mewed all night. My mother refused to even touch it, but my father listened to our neighbor's instructions and accepted the cans of formula and an eye dropper.

The kitten was blind, as newborn kittens are, and fit into the palm of my father's hand. He fed it with the eye dropper, the kitten cupped in his hand and resting against his stomach.

My mother named it Sambo, my father called it Rambo.

Rambo grew up to be a huge, sleek cat, who attacked and bit everyone except my father. I guess no one else had the touch. I once watched my father pet Rambo and was surprised that Rambo's fur stayed on.

X.

The flats of lotus stretched out to span ten acres, bordered on either side by the lush green of neighboring watercress. The once vibrant green lotus leaves were turning brown, curling inward.

Kam Ngao stood knee deep in mud, thigh deep in water, swatting at the biting flies and cursing. The field did not drain—not only did he have to dig deep into the mud, but the few inches of water standing above the mud would make more work. Hopefully the roots would not be deep. Otherwise he'd have to feel around with his feet and risk breaking the long tubers.

After hacking at the rough stalk and throwing the leaves onto the bank, he followed the stalk down into the mud with his hands, turning his face before it touched the muddy water. Ngao could feel the bump of the root extending to the right, and he quickly dug at the layers of mud at the surface, forming a channel over the anticipated tuber growth. Gently, he began to dig around the sides of the root, using his forearms to hold back the mud collapsing back over the root. At the same time he carefully disentangled the keiki roots to put aside for replanting. When the long segmented lotus root was free of the weight and grip of the soil, it floated to the surface.

After the harvested lotus roots had been washed and cleaned, Yook Fa could sell them—for three cents a pound.

XI.

Every Tuesday my father and I would visit Popo. We'd stop at Kamehameha Shopping Center to buy ground beef and bread. Popo made excellent "hamburgers"—she would mix together beef, old bread, green onions, eggs and milk and then fry the patties.

My father would turn down Tom "Dynamite" Dancer and ask the usual questions as Popo cooked. I would look through the many family picture albums.

Shortly after Popo's second husband died, all the albums containing pictures of Popo's first family disappeared. Albums containing pictures of the children and grandchildren and great-grandchildren from the second family remained, however. I never mentioned this to my father, but I did stop looking through the albums, and visited less frequently.

XII.

Kam Ngao had mastered the art of mongoose trapping. Using a wooden box propped up with a stick and a long string tied to that stick, Ngao baited the trap by cracking an egg under the angled box. He then hid, the length of string carefully pulled so there was no slack, and waited.

227

Once caught, the mongoose would provide the day's entertainment. It would be bagged, its fighting body subdued by the press of a piece of wood, and its leg drawn out of the bag. Swiftly then, Ngao would hammer the mongoose's leg to a two by four.

Then he'd let the dogs loose.

XIII.

Clarence Kam Ngao Wong lay propped up in the hospital bed doing respiratory therapy, which consisted of blowing into a tube so three blue plastic balls could be carried by his breath. it was a ridiculous thing to do, his chest hurt, but the respiratory therapist was cute. And it was the doctor's orders.

His wife entered, the crease between her eyebrows deepened from the waiting, waiting for him during the bypass, waiting to see if his strength would return.

"The doctor says you're doing good."

"He tol' me fo' stop chasing the nurses; no good fo' my heart, bumbye I get one 'notha heart attack."

"Clarence! Really." His wife smiled, and the crease softened. She gripped his fingers tightly.

XIV.

One thing I forgot to mention about my father and I. We look very much alike. Everyone said so when I was growing up. My father and I would hold our hands out, palms up, next to each other. My hands looked exactly like his, only smaller.

Translation of Cantonese terms

api in: opium
nam mo: priest
ngao: ox *or* lotus root
yup pun chai: Japanese

Contributors Notes

Beryl Blaich (b. 1946): "I am Hawaiian Chinese English Irish. I know little of these roots, especially of my mother's family, the Hawaiian-Chinese Kaopuas. Nothing of my grandfather. Of my grandmother, Kamila Amina Kaopua, just a couple of jottings, pencilled on separate pages, into a tiny leather-bound notebook, hard to make out. 'My father died December 5, 1918 Look sai.' Or is it Took sai or Fook tai? And 'Ana Kalama b. August 16, 1864, Mama, died April 17, 1921.' A Chinese great grandfather. A Hawaiian great grandmother. My mother often recalls of her mother, who died at about the age of 42 in 1930, that she loved and regularly played mah-jongg."

Joseph S.M.J. Chang (b. 1923): "I am an Associate Professor of English at the University of Wisconsin-Milwaukee, teaching courses in Shakespeare and in Film Studies. My Ph.D. is from Wisconsin, and my dissertation was on Shakespeare. I have five children, all reared on the mainland, who have scant acquaintance with Hawaii, and so what I wrote was as much for them as for my siblings, this attempt to remember what it was like, growing up Chinese in Hawaii.

I have no specific awareness of how my (relatively) exotic background influences my professional life. Most of my students eventually get to know that I am from Hawaii. I leave it to them to figure out how my being Chinese-Hawaiian alters my point of view. I do not try to teach a Chinese Shakespeare, any more than I try to teach an Elizabethan Shakespeare. Like him, I have to live my life in the age I am trapped in.

Still, I am conscious of my special role in that part of academia which has long been dominated by WASPs. For an Asian to be teaching Shakespeare remains a small wonder, and I am aware that black students look to me for some moral support. It is an unspoken pact between us. While I was Coordinator of Graduate Studies, it was important to me to recruit the Department's first Chinese-American Ph.D. student (as opposed to Chinese nationals who would return to either Taiwan or the PRC). So you might say that I am aware of a responsibility in enlarging the spheres in which all minorities can participate in American society."

Phoebe Chun Chang (1909-1972) was born in Sam Heong (Ping Larm), Chung Shan, China. Her parents brought her to Hawaii around age two. Always a good student, she declined to go back to China because her studies would suffer. Of course, she later regretted this youthful enthusiasm. She graduated from UH with a teaching degree in 1931 and taught in Laupahoehoe, Molokai and rural Oahu schools before settling at Farrington High School. She started out teaching math, then core studies. In the 1960's, when there was a national push to teach foreign languages, she was granted fellowships to attend Mandarin language institutes in Seton Hall, New Jersey and in Taiwan. She then taught Mandarin at Farrington. She retired from Farrington High School several years before she died of cancer in 1972.

Thomas M.C. Chang (b. 1923) is the oldest of eight children born to Chang Koon Kwai and Lum Sam Chang. The others are Francis, Henry, Anita, Ronnie, Barbara, and Joseph. A sister died in infancy. Tom is married to Vivian A.C. Ching. They have two sons, David Alan and Williamson. Tom is retired from the University of Hawaii-Manoa. Vivian is retired from the Department of Education.

Laureen Ching (b. 1951) no longer writes poetry. Under her real name Laureen Kwock, her short fiction has appeared in *Hawaii Review, AsiAm, Chaminade Literary Review,* and *South Dakota Review.* Her novels appear under the pen name of Clarice Peters.

Eric Chock (b. 1950) is a local poet.

Sue Lin Chong (b. 1948): "Even though I was born in Hawaii, my family moved to two different places in the Mainland between my first and fifth birthdays. And when I turned six, we "permanently" moved from Hawaii to New Jersey. I am happy to have returned and lived in Hawaii these past thirteen years. Initially my motivation was to learn more about my relatives and being Chinese among a larger ethnic population, grow in my career, and enjoy the sunshine. Learning about my relatives and history has been infinitely rewarding and brought me unexpected delights—the other things turned out to be important, but not nearly as important as the first goal. For one thing, I only recently have come to appreciate the wit, creativity, and thoughts of my maternal grandfather, as revealed through his writings to his friends and family. I would like to think this spirit can be further passed along to others through my own writing."

Herbert K.K. Chun (b. 1955) lives in Honolulu.

James H. Chun (b. 1901) graduated from McKinley High School in 1924 and the University of Hawaii in 1928. While at the University, he was very active despite a heavy working schedule: President of Chinese Students Alliance; president of Chinese Students Club; secretary of Hawaii Union; editor of Chinese Students Alliance Annual; editor of Ka Palapala, the University yearbook. He later worked at the *Honolulu Star Bulletin*, Honolulu Trust Company, Ltd., and Dean Witter and Company while remaining active in Chinese community organizations. He helped organize the Hawaii Chinese Civic Association and served for many years as an editor and director of the organization.

Sheryl Dare (b. 1948): "I'm the dance reviewer for the *Honolulu Advertiser* and am currently working on a novel for Macmillan publishers."

Bessie C. Lai (b. 1900), now 89 years old, is still a firm believer in her Chinese religious beliefs and practices. Every morning without fail, this pious woman burns incense sticks and asks her goddess Kwan Yin to bless and fortify her throughout the day.

Li Ling-Ai (b. circa 1910): "I am deeply delighted and surprised that you have discovered a very early piece of one of my literary endeavors written when I was a young student in Hawaii showing the conflicts of cultures.

But I am more pleased to know that the editors have been publishing *Bamboo Ridge Press* since 1978 and have initiated the project to encourage writings from Chinese Americans to perhaps reveal the classicism of their heritage and that of America and thereby add richness, depth, and understanding to our existence, which was the intent, I suspect, of such men as Ben Franklin, John Quincy Adams, and Thomas Jefferson when they wrote the Constitution.

Yours will then be a singular service, as were the strivings of my own parents and the early immigrants from China, to add to the richness of human concepts not only of Hawaii but of America."

Charlotte Lum (b. 1923): "On re-reading the script, I felt again the sense of a kind of loneliness of lives that tended to each develop cocoon-like. It was not that family members were uncaring of each other, but that here was a group of people who were undemonstrative in their most tender feelings and tended to communicate superficially. There is a stripping away of outer layers to touch the inner selves of others in the daughter's mind so as to underscore a bonding before leaving.

Ethnicity was not a focal point in delineating those characters. Being undemonstrative, stoic, and having generational differences are not exclusive properties of the Chinese. Indeed, the inference is that these are some ways the Chinese are so like many other human beings anywhere in the world."

Darrell H.Y. Lum (b. 1950) serves as co-editor of *Bamboo Ridge, The Hawaii Writers' Quarterly*, husband to Mae Amy, and daddy to Lisa Terumi Kwai Oi Lum and Daniel Jordan Senjiro Wing Keong Lum.

Wing Tek Lum's (b. 1946) first collection of poetry, *Expounding the Doubtful Points*, was published by *Bamboo Ridge Press* in 1987.

Cathy Song (b. 1955) is the author of *Picture Bride* (Yale) and *Frameless Windows, Squares of Light* (Norton).

Susan Lee St. John (b. 1956) was born and raised in Hawaii, although for the past 13 years she has lived in Oregon. She and her husband recently returned to the islands, and she now teaches at St. Andrew's Priory. Her work has also appeared in *The Forbidden Stitch: An Asian American Women's Anthology*. She received her M.F.A. from the University of Oregon in 1988.

Reuben Tam (b. 1916), Kauai-born painter and poet, studied at the University of Hawaii, Columbia University, and the New School for Social Research. After a long residency in New York City where he painted and exhibited, he returned to his hometown of Kapaa in 1980. His poems have appeared in many literary journals and anthologies. He was a finalist in the 1988 National Poetry Competition of the Chester H. Jones Foundation. He recently won the Cades Award.

Wai Chee Chun Yee (b. 1917): Originally included in a typescript volume of undergraduate student plays, "For You a Lei" was written for Willard Wilson's drama writing course in The One-Act Play during the first semester of 1936-37. Because he was "convinced that many of the plays deserved a better fate than the oblivion of a student's notebook..." he "gathered together this cross-section of student thinking...and...had the examples bound together for the library of the University of Hawaii."

With its "resurrection" after more than a half a century, "For You a Lei" is now considered by some Asian American literature researchers as the earliest example of the use of pidgin in writing. The first reading of a scene from the play was presented by the Rainbow Interpretation Organization (RIO) at a workshop of "Literary Pioneers..." at the *Lucky Come Hawaii: The Chinese in Hawaii* Conference held in Jefferson Hall, East-West Center, on July 20, 1988. RIO is affiliated with the Interpretation Studies Program of the Department of Speech, U.H.-Manoa.

Wai Chee Chun (Mrs. Jewett Yee) is a retired catalog librarian and assistant library specialist at Hamilton Library, University of Hawaii, where she also served as the Library Ombudsman. She is a 1934 graduate of Punahou School, the University of Hawaii in 1937, and the School of Library Service of Columbia University, New York, in 1939.

Doug Young (b. 1951) is a local photo-realist watercolor painter who has had numerous one-man and group shows in Hawaii and the mainland. His Chinatown series, featured in this book, was done in the early 70s at the time when Chinatown was in turmoil because of housing evictions and redevelopment.

Kathleen Ngit Jun Young (b. 1964): "Our pasts do not return to us whole. Instead they burst upon us like a scattering of mirror shards and whatever reflective integration they possess is not given but composed by virtue of the positionings of consciousness. "Digging for Lotus Roots" presents seemingly isolated, but emotionally related scenes, which the reader can render coherent only by creating a narrative that unifies them as parts of a life which are necessarily his or her own, and not that of a disembodied, ahistorical author."

Dana Leilehua Yuen (b. 1958): "It is easier to wash rice in a rice-basket than in an aluminum pot."

Acknowledgments

Some of the work appearing in this volume was previously published in the following publications:

Beryl Blaich, "Apparition," *Chaminade Literary Review,* no. 3, Fall 1988.

Phoebe Chun Chang, "Li Po in Hawaii," *Chinese Students' Alliance Annual XII,* 1929.

Laureen Ching, "Fever," *Hawaii Review* #17, Spring 1985.

Eric Chock, "The Mango Tree," *Bamboo Ridge* #4, Bamboo Ridge Press, September-November 1979.
"Poem for My Father," *Wind,* The Wind Press, vol. 7, no. 27, 1977.
"Chinese New Year," *San Marcos Review*, vol. 7, no. 2, San Marcos Press, 1978.

Herbert K.K. Chun, "Pa-ke," *The Best of Bamboo Ridge*, 1986, originally from *Bamboo Ridge* #3, Bamboo Ridge Press, June 1979.

James H. Chun, "In the Camp," *Chinese Students' Alliance Annual VI*, 1923.

Sheryl Dare, "Sleeper," *Hapa* #2, Spring 1982.
"For Tom 1945-1975," *Poetry Hawaii*, University Press of Hawaii, 1979.

Bessie C. Lai, excerpt from *Ah Yā, I Still Remember, Ah Yā, I Still Remember*, Meadea Enterprise Co., Inc., Taipei, Taiwan, 1926.

Li Ling-Ai, "The Submission of Rose Moy," *Hawaii Quill Magazine*, vol. 1, no. 2, June 1928.

Charlotte Lum, "These Unsaid Things," *College Plays,* (University of Hawaii Department of English, 1948-1949), vol. IV.

Darrell H.Y. Lum, "J'like Ten Thousand," *Landmarks, Magazine of Northwest History and Preservation,* vol. IV, No. 3 & 4, 1986, Seattle.

Wing Tek Lum, "Juk," "T-Bone Steak," "Chinese Hot Pot," "The Poet Imagines His Grandfather on the Day He Died," *Expounding the Doubtful Points,* Bamboo Ridge Press, 1987. "Kindergarten," *Bamboo Ridge* #36, Bamboo Ridge Press, Fall 1987.
"Poetic License," *Bamboo Ridge* #41, Bamboo Ridge Press, Winter 1989.

Cathy Song, "A Pale Arrangement of Hands," *Picture Bride,* Yale University Press, 1983, reprinted with permission. "Living Near the Water," "Shadow Figures," "The Tower of Pisa," "Heaven," reprinted from *Frameless Windows, Squares of Light,* Poems by Cathy Song, by permission of the author and the publisher, W.W. Norton & Company, Inc. Copyright© 1988 by Cathy Song.

Reuben Tam, "Ghost Dogs of Halaula," *Chaminade Literary Review No. 3,* Fall 1988.

Wai Chee Chun Yee, "For You a Lei," *College Plays,* (University of Hawaii Department of English, 1937), vol. 1.

Kathleen Ngit Jun Young, "Digging for Lotus Roots," *Hawaii Review,* Issue 27, vol. 13, no. 3, Fall 1989.